All Hands In?
Making Diversity Work for All

))OECD

This work is published under the responsibility of the Secretary-General of the OECD. The opinions expressed and arguments employed herein do not necessarily reflect the official views of OECD member countries.

This document, as well as any data and map included herein, are without prejudice to the status of or sovereignty over any territory, to the delimitation of international frontiers and boundaries and to the name of any territory, city or area.

The statistical data for Israel are supplied by and under the responsibility of the relevant Israeli authorities. The use of such data by the OECD is without prejudice to the status of the Golan Heights, East Jerusalem and Israeli settlements in the West Bank under the terms of international law.

Please cite this publication as:
OECD (2020), *All Hands In? Making Diversity Work for All*, OECD Publishing, Paris, *https://doi.org/10.1787/efb14583-en*.

ISBN 978-92-64-60063-8 (print)
ISBN 978-92-64-47222-8 (pdf)

Foreword

The year 2020 has started with COVID-19 pandemic becoming the most severe human health crisis in a century, and this has quickly turned into the biggest economic crisis since the Second World War. The depth and reach of this crisis has exposed once again existing inequalities in our economies and societies and risks further widening them. Older people and many people with disabilities are facing elevated COVID-19 health risks, but, in many countries, ethnic minorities are also disproportionately more likely to die than the majority population. The disease is also affecting disproportionally migrants, partly because they have restricted access to health care, but also because they may live and work in conditions where social distancing is hard to enforce. A further reason, common to many different social minorities, is that a lifetime of disadvantage and low social status, leaves them more vulnerable to disease than mainstream groups.

Minority groups are often in more unstable and vulnerable positions in the labour market and the current COVID-19 crisis has hit them disproportionally hard. When in employment, they often hold more precarious and unstable jobs, which often give weaker or no access to social protection compared to those offered by standard jobs during the crisis. A disproportionate share of women and migrants, in particular, are also employed in sectors that have been either on the front line – like health care sector – exposing them to the associated risks of contracting the virus, or particularly hard-hit by the strict confinement measures, like hotel and restaurants.

This report was prepared before the onset of the COVID-19 pandemic, but it addresses many of the issues the disease has laid bare. Indeed, with COVID-19, there is a real risk that the significant progress obtained over the past decade in promoting a fuller role in labour markets and society of diverse groups will be at least partially lost. We cannot afford to let this happen. Moreover, since this report was prepared, the death of George Floyd and the global "Black Lives Matter" movement have placed at the centre of the policy debate long-standing issues of persistent discrimination and disadvantage against ethnic minorities into the limelight. The report also addresses these issues.

A number of lessons can be drawn from the analysis in this report that are particularly relevant in the current unprecedented crisis. A first key lesson is that excluding diverse populations from the labour market comes at a high economic and social cost that countries can ill afford – especially in such challenging times. While there are strong societal and macroeconomic benefits of including diverse groups, action towards greater inclusion of diverse groups cannot be left only to individual businesses. As many businesses are struggling and layoffs increase, we need to make sure that the incentives for fair and equal treatment for all are well set. Evidence suggests that discrimination becomes more pronounced when unemployment rises.

A second key lesson is that there is a need to continuously monitor the evolving situation for diverse groups. Only if facts are fully at hand, it is possible for policy makers and other key stakeholders to adequately react. It is also important to look at 'intersectionality' (when people are part of multiple minority groups), to make sure that the most vulnerable are not neglected.

A third core lesson of our report is that effective mainstreaming of diversity requires a "diversity lens" by which the impact of policy measures on diverse groups is considered prior to implementation. As countries design and implement policies to cope with the crisis, and to create a better 'new normal', their impact on diverse groups needs to be assessed up front.

While the immediate priority during the pandemic was, and still is, to contain the spread of the virus and save lives, policy makers are now also facing the daunting challenge of managing the economic recovery from a deep recession to avoid massive unemployment and increases in poverty and exclusion. Managing the recovery requires a focus on diverse groups so as to avoid further inequalities and instead better exploiting the full potential of a more diverse and equal economy and society so as to make them more resilient. Getting the most out of our increasingly diverse societies is not a fair weather issue, it is, on the contrary, now more essential than ever.

Stefano Scarpetta
Director for Employment, Labour and Social Affairs
Organisation for Economic Co-operation and Development

Acknowledgements

Additional funding was provided through the OECD's Central Priority Fund (CPF) to support a new area of work on the economic impact of diversity, and the appropriate policy responses to making the most of diverse societies. This document presents the findings of this work. The report was prepared by Shirin Abrishami Kashani and Eva Degler under the supervision of Thomas Liebig, all from the OECD's International Migration Division, and under the leadership of Mark Pearson, Deputy Director for Employment, Labour and Social Affairs. It benefitted from comments by Willem Adema, Carlotta Balestra, Stephane Carcillo, Jean-Christophe Dumont, Lara Fleischer, Marco Mira D'Ercole, Natalia Nolan Flecha, Christopher Prinz, Monika Queisser, Stefano Scarpetta and Marie-Anne Valfort. Chapter 3 benefitted from a background report by Ceren Ozgen (Marie Sklodowska-Curie Fellow at the Department of Economics and the Institute for Research into Superdiversity (IRiS) at the University of Birmingham). The report also includes a contribution by Martyna Wanat, from the OECD's Directorate for Public Governance. Liv Gudmundson, Natalie Corry and Lucy Hullet prepared the publication.

The report includes results from a survey among 2400 HR managers in eight OECD countries that was conducted together with the Chair Management, Diversités et Cohésion Sociale of Paris Dauphine University and with the support of national Human Ressource (HR) Associations to gather evidence on the experiences and views of HR professionals regarding diversity practices in their firms. The Secretariat would like to thank Jean-François Chanlat, Mustafa Özbilgin and Maria Giuseppina Bruna for the the co-operation, as well as the supporting HR Associations: Australian HR Institute (AHRI), Chartered Professionals in Human Resources (CPHR, Canada) and Human Resources Professionals Association (HRPA, Canada), Association Nationale des DRH (ANDRH, France), Deutsche Gesellschaft für Personalführung (DGFP, Germany), Associazione Italiana per la Direzione del Personale (AIDP, Italy), HR Norge (Norway), Associação Portuguesa de Gestão das Pessoas (APG, Portugal) and Fundación para el Desarrollo de la Función de Recursos Humanos Fundipe (Spain).

The report also builds on the results of a policy questionnaire that was sent to member countries through the delegates of the Employment, Labour and Social Affairs Committee. The Secretariat would like to thank the Delegates for their support, as well as for their comments on the report.

Table of contents

Tables

Figures

Boxes

Follow OECD Publications on:

http://twitter.com/OECD_Pubs

http://www.facebook.com/OECDPublications

http://www.linkedin.com/groups/OECD-Publications-4645871

http://www.youtube.com/oecdilibrary

http://www.oecd.org/oecddirect/

Executive summary

This report considers five key groups who are widely considered disadvantaged in the labour market and who often face discrimination based on their group membership: immigrants, their descendants and ethnic minorities; LGBT people; older people; people with disabilities; and women.

OECD labour markets and societies have become increasingly diverse over the past decades. For example, shares of immigrants and their children have increased in virtually all OECD countries; more people are open about their sexual orientation than ever before; and the share of women in the labour force has increased often markedly. Awareness for issues surrounding diversity has also increased: in 2018, an overwhelming majority out of the 2 400 Human Resource (HR) professionals surveyed by the OECD in collaboration with national HR associations agreed that in the previous five years, the topic of diversity had gained more attention in their country (85%) and in their companies specifically (65%).

Ensuring that OECD countries are equipped to make the most of diversity by fully utilising all talent among diverse populations and promoting inclusive labour markets and societies is a key challenge ahead. Both businesses and governments are responding to this challenge with policies to strengthen the inclusion of diverse populations at the workplace and in the labour market in general. This report assesses: i) how labour market inclusion of women and minority groups in OECD countries has evolved over time; ii) the evidence on how diversity affects economic outcomes; and iii) which policies countries have implemented and what is known about their effectiveness.

While there has been some progress, there is a long way to go to achieve full inclusion

Recent trends suggest some margin of optimism regarding the attitudes towards women and minority groups. Attitudes towards gender equality and LGBT people, for example, have become more favourable in OECD countries over the past ten years. In addition, labour market outcomes have improved on many fronts. Employment gaps between men and women and between older and prime-age workers have decreased considerably. In two out of three OECD countries, gaps for both groups decreased by at least 25% between 2007 and 2017. At the same time, however, attitudes towards migrants and ethnic minorities have become more polarised.

In any event, the full economic and social inclusion of disadvantaged groups remains an elusive goal. Progress on labour market outcomes is uneven and in most countries, substantial gaps remain not only for women and older workers, but also for people with disabilities and for migrants and their children. Furthermore, only a small majority of people in the OECD (55%) believe their neighbourhoods are good places to live for ethnic minorities, LGBT people and immigrants.

COVID-19 has exposed that women and minorities are not only more exposed to health risks, but also in a more vulnerable situation in the labour market. They are often in more precarious and unstable forms of employment, which in some cases has left them without or with weak access to social protection. A disproportionate share of women and migrants, in particular, are also employed in certain sectors such as hotel and restaurants which have been particularly hard-hit.

There are evident economic and social gains from better inclusion, whereas the business case for diversity is less evident

Besides the obligation to ensure inclusion rooted in social justice, excluding diverse populations from the labour market comes at a high cost. Much could be gained by fully utilising and developing the potential of disadvantaged groups in the labour market and society at large – especially in the context of population ageing. While there is thus a strong macroeconomic case for diversity, the business case for more diversity is less clear-cut. Existing research at the firm level has largely focused on assessing the impact of foreign-born workers and women on firm productivity and innovation. While the impact of diversity on firm performance tends to be positive and higher in knowledge-intensive, high-skilled, and innovation-driven sectors, it may not be in other sectors.

However, studies which focus on outcomes provide little insight about the processes behind how diversity is managed on a day-to-day basis. Finding that diversity does not boost productivity in some sectors might be because companies have not yet found ways to effectively bring together different perspectives, ideas and networks to maximise the potential of their diverse workforce. Making the most of diversity is not a simple 'numbers game' of increasing staff diversity, but depends on whether employees feel respected and valued, how discriminatory actions are sanctioned, and what incentives and policies are put in place to foster equality of opportunity.

OECD countries have implemented a wide range of diversity policies and strategies

Most countries have gone beyond anti-discrimination legislation and implemented additional diversity measures, recognising that anti-discrimination policy alone cannot remove structural obstacles for disadvantaged groups. While it is important to fully implement this legislation, making the most of the diversity of our societies cannot be done by only focussing only on what people and companies should *not* do but also promote pro-active efforts by all stakeholders.

Given the fact that promoting diversity at the firm level is not always straightforward, many governments seek to strengthen the business case for companies. Most OECD countries reward firms' commitment to diversity with labels and awards. In addition, many countries provide financial incentives, e.g. subsidies and tax breaks, to firms that hire certain diverse and/or disadvantaged job candidates and promote supplier diversity in public procurement policies. Over the past ten years, European countries, in particular, have gone beyond positive incentives for firms to foster diversity by introducing quotas for specific sectors or positions, mostly for women and people with disabilities. Furthermore, the majority of OECD countries have implemented diversity strategies to increase representation of various disadvantaged groups in public administration.

Existing frameworks must better differentiate the needs of diverse groups

Despite the variety of instruments in place, whether diversity policies actually work in practice and why is still under-researched. This is partly due to few countries evaluating or monitoring the impact of existing policies. Yet, understanding "what works" for which groups and why is crucial. Evidence suggests that existing diversity measures often disregard the considerable heterogeneity both between and within groups and consequently have unequal effects on diverse populations. For example, evidence shows that affirmative action programmes in the United States have benefitted white women more than ethnic minorities. Quota regulations, which have proven effective in getting more women in corporate boards, can be counterproductive when applied to other groups, such as people with disabilities. Such findings demonstrate that there are group-specific barriers, which cannot be addressed through "one-size-fits-all" diversity policies.

Crucially, most existing diversity policies tend to neglect socio-economic disadvantage. Studies on access to higher education suggest that diversity policies primarily benefit the most privileged within an ethnic minority group, e.g. those from families with relatively high incomes or high levels of education. While the principle of equal opportunities should apply to people of any socio-economic background and status, policies fail to help the most disadvantaged within minority groups will not end injustice. Finally, policy makers have to face the danger that disadvantaged individuals who do not happen to fall into the category of any particular "diverse group" may feel left out and discriminated against. Diversity policies, therefore, can only be one part of a broader package of policies to promote equal opportunities among all members of society.

Against this backdrop, the following lists summarise some key actions that have been identified as crucial for effective corporate and public policy in making the most of diverse societies. For some specific groups – women, people with disabilities, and older workers – the OECD Council has approved targeted recommendations.

Actions for employers seeking to make the most of a diverse workforce

Action 1: Communicate clearly about the rationale for diversity policies

- Counter the persistent misconception that diversity policies only benefit women and minorities and come at the detriment of majority groups by showing how they can benefit everyone.
- Maintain that diversity is not an end in itself, but that the ultimate objective is to strengthen equality of opportunity by 'widening the gate' rather than lowering the bar.

Action 2: Reach out to potential applicants from diverse backgrounds and encourage them to apply to jobs

- Invest in outreach to groups who are under-represented in a given sector or job field and who may not have the necessary professional networks, e.g. by organising targeted job fairs and recruitment campaigns.

Action 3: Develop comprehensive diversity strategies

- Develop diversity action plans targeting recruitment but also retention and career progression to ensure a comprehensive approach towards diversity in the workplace.
- Ensure that these strategies contain quantifiable goals, commitment from upper management and mechanisms to ensure accountability for targets.

Action 4: Tackle discrimination in the hiring process and in the workplace

- Ensure equality of opportunity in recruitment by tackling discrimination and unconscious bias, setting up diverse selection teams and interview panels, and strengthening recourse mechanisms for potential victims of discrimination.
- Support internal staff networks that promote diversity and inclusion as they can represent the interest of groups better.

Action 5: Consider intersectionality in diversity management

- Recognise that people have multiple identities that are necessarily more complex than the simplified categorisations often used for practical purposes. For example, disadvantages experienced by ethnic minority women differ from those of white women or ethnic minority men.

Action 6: Ensure broader and more equitable access to diversity measures

- Target disadvantage within groups, e.g. socio-economic status or position within firm hierarchy, to avoid that policies predominantly benefit those in a relatively privileged position.

Action 7: Acknowledge and address possible negative reactions

- Include all staff, regardless of their background, in developing and implementing diversity policies and gather regular employee feedback on diversity policies.
- Recognise that negative reactions do not necessarily arise because diversity policies fail, as social change is often accompanied by conflict.

A 10-point checklist for public action to get the most out of diverse societies

1. Raise awareness of non-discrimination legislation and recourse mechanisms and make sure that these are accessible and effectively protect potential victims from retaliation.

2. Make sure that the public sector is a role model in diversity management and that it adequately reflects the diversity of the society it represents.

3. Ensure broader and more equitable access to diversity measures by considering socio-economic disadvantage within groups and avoiding that policies predominantly benefit those in a relatively privileged position.

4. Develop diversity policies that focus on all jobs, with a particular attention to medium- and low-skilled jobs.

5. Acknowledge that diversity policies are not a 'quick fix' to tackle inequalities and frame them as part of a broader approach, notably with respect to improving access to quality education and lifelong learning.

6. Find the right balance between general and group-specific policies and consider the possible stigmatising effects of the latter, as well as the negative repercussions that can result from inadequate choice of terminology in designating the group.

7. Anticipate possible negative reactions towards diversity and develop a proactive communication strategy, also working with other stakeholders, that frames diversity policies within a wider context of equal opportunities for all members of society.

8. Strengthen the business case for diversity, including through appropriate incentives and by ensuring that hiring disadvantaged groups does not incur disproportionate costs for employers.

9. Support companies, notably SMEs, in their efforts to diversify their staff, for example by providing concrete "how-to" guides and "diversity consultants".

10. Improve data collection on diverse groups in the labour market, including at firm level, to facilitate a better monitoring of the effectiveness of public policies and to identify areas where further policy action is needed.

1 Diversity in OECD countries: Population diversity, labour market inclusion and acceptance of diversity

This chapter provides an overview of how diverse OECD populations are, taking into consideration the population shares of foreign-born, native-born with immigrant parents, older people and people with disabilities. In addition, it presents a Migrant Diversity Index that reflects both the size of migrant populations as well as the heterogeneity within them. To provide an indication of how countries are faring in terms of labour market inclusion, the chapter presents a dashboard showing how employment gaps for minority groups and women have evolved over time. Lastly, it discusses how acceptance of diversity in the OECD has changed over time, provides an overview of perceived discrimination levels and presents findings on public support for diversity policies in the work place.

OECD countries and, by extension, their labour force, have become considerably more diverse in a rather short timeframe. Over the past two decades, the labour market participation of women has increased strongly; the population shares of migrants and their children are growing in almost all OECD countries and more LGBT people are open about their sexual orientation. These societal changes are occurring against the backdrop of ageing societies and a larger share of older workers than in past decades.

Ensuring that these groups are included in the labour market is therefore a key policy concern, not only for ethical reasons, but also in terms of economic development and social cohesion. In this context, the office of the OECD Secretary General allocated resources of the Central Priorities Fund (CPF) to assess how OECD countries can be equipped to make the most out of diversity and ensure equality of opportunity. Based on long-standing work by the OECD on groups traditionally disadvantaged in the labour market, a policy questionnaire among OECD countries on diversity policies as well as an online survey among HR professionals, this report addresses the question of how governments and businesses can set the conditions to make the most out of a diverse workforce.

The term 'diversity' is used as an umbrella term and in this report focuses on five overlapping groups that are widely seen as being disadvantaged and discriminated against in the labour market; women; immigrants, their descendants and ethnic minorities; LGBT people; older people; and people with disabilities. By its very nature, the choice of groups to include is challenging. Young people, for example, are disadvantaged in many countries, but are not included here since they are rarely included in national legislation listing groups against whom discrimination is prohibited, whereas the five groups listed above are, in most cases. Furthermore, while it may seem surprising to classify women as a diverse group – given that they represent half of the population – they are nevertheless included in this overview, reflecting both persisting inequalities in the labour market as well as the fact that diversity policies have long focused on providing equal opportunities for women. Finally, while this report analyses existing policies targeting certain groups that share common traits, it is equally important to acknowledge the influence that interactions of multiple advantages and disadvantages can have on individuals' outcomes.

The report first discusses under which conditions diversity in the workforce may present a 'business case' for firms or the economy at large and presents evidence on how diversity can affect social cohesion more broadly. Chapter 3 shows how population diversity and labour market participation of women and minority groups in OECD countries have evolved over time. In addition, it provides an overview of attitudes towards diversity, equality and diversity policies and demonstrates how they have evolved. Chapter 4 evaluates some of the key existing diversity instruments, including both public policies and corporate practices, connects it with evidence on their effectiveness and, where possible, discusses differential effects on groups. Chapter 5 highlights the key challenges faced by governments and employers and Chapter 6 concludes.

Population diversity in OECD countries

Diversity is a broad term and includes many groups for which data are not available or are difficult to compare across countries or, in many cases, between different government agencies and data sources (e.g. household surveys, administrative data) in the same country. This is notably the case for ethnic identity (Box 1.1) as well as for LGBT people. Only a few population-based surveys include questions on sexual orientation and even within a given country, shares can differ markedly depending on whether survey questions ask for sexual self-identification or sexual behaviour and whether they are administered online or face-to-face (Valfort, 2017[1]). For example, estimates of the LGB population in the United States vary between 2.8% and 5.6%. For gender identity, Chile, Denmark and the United States have started to implement representative surveys on the transgender population (Balestra and Fleischer, 2018[2]). The following therefore looks at four dimensions of population diversity that can be more easily defined and compared across countries – the share of foreign-born, natives with at least one immigrant parent, older people, and people with disabilities (Table 1.1).

Box 1.1. Ethnic identity and statistics

There has been a long-standing debate in a number of OECD countries on whether data on ethnicity should be collected and how these data should then be used. Better data on diversity, including ethnic and indigenous identity, will be key to understanding the size, outcomes and needs of different communities, to make them statistically visible and in turn implement effective diversity policies. The collection practices of National Statistical Offices on ethnic identity data generally cluster around three broad categories (Balestra and Fleischer, 2018[2]):

- All OECD countries collect information on ethnicity proxies such as country of birth (36 OECD members);
- A small majority, mostly Eastern European countries as well as the United Kingdom, Ireland, the United States, Canada and Australia gather additional information on race and ethnicity (16 OECD members);
- Only a handful of countries in the Americas and Oceania collect data on indigenous identity (6 OECD members).

A major challenge to expanding ethnicity data collection, particularly in older EU member states, are restrictive legal frameworks that govern the treatment of (historically) sensitive data. Nevertheless, a considerable majority of EU citizens (70%) would be in favour of providing information on their ethnic origin as part of the census. Support is lowest in Hungary, Slovenia and Poland (around 50%) and highest in Sweden and Denmark (80-90%) (Eurobarometer, 2015[3]).

A recent review of data collection practices around the OECD, also part of the OECD Diversity project, serves as a toolbox for interested data producers to gather reliable information on ethnic identity in their own countries going forward (Balestra and Fleischer, 2018[2]). The review gives examples on how to tackle the challenges of ensuring respondent privacy, and optimising comparability of data over time when collective identities, and sometimes the corresponding response categories in questionnaires, change in line with societal trends. For instance, there have been a growing number of United States respondents who do not identify with any of the official race categories in the Census, and whom have been racially classified as "Some Other Race", which was initially intended to be a small residual category (Bureau, 2018[4]). In addition, ensuring comparability of ethnic self-identification over time and creating valid and reliable statistical categories can be a challenge. For example, in the United States census people of Middle Eastern or North African (MENA) descent are included in the ethnic category 'white'. Research indicates that with an inclusion of a distinct MENA category, close to 80% of respondents identified as MENA indeed choose the option MENA and around 20% choose the category 'white'. If no MENA answer option is provided, 85% choose 'white' and 12% 'some other race' (Mathews et al., 2017[5]). These differences highlight how answering options can affect how people identify and what subsequently gets measured as ethnic diversity.

Table 1.1 shows considerable differences in population diversity across OECD countries. In about a quarter of OECD countries, immigrants make up less than 3.5% of the total population, whereas in eight OECD countries shares exceed 18%. Consequently, in countries with low immigrant shares, the population size of natives with at least one immigrant parent are also small, whereas the opposite is true for countries with high shares of immigrants.

For older people within working age, shares of the total working age population range between 10% and 20% in OECD countries. Shares of people in EU countries who report having a disability fall between 14% and 25%. Table 1.1 also shows that relatively few countries score high in more than two of the dimensions shown below.

In Poland, the Slovak Republic and Hungary, for instance, the share of immigrants and the share of natives with at least one immigrant parent are among the lowest in the OECD, while for older workers they rank among the highest.

Table 1.1. Population diversity in OECD countries, 2017 (or nearest year)

Share of total population, except for older people and people with disabilities

Foreign-born		Native-born with at least one foreign-born parent		55-64 year-olds (15-64 population)		People with disabilities (15+ population)	
0.3-3.4%	Poland	0.2-2.1%	Korea	10.4-17.8%	Mexico	13.6-16.1%	
	Mexico		Japan		Turkey		France
	Slovak Republic		Mexico		Israel		Czech Republic
	Hungary		Turkey		Chile		Italy
	Japan		Chile		Luxembourg		Portugal
	Turkey		Hungary		Ireland		Sweden
	Korea		Slovak Republic		Australia		Luxembourg
	Chile		Greece		Norway		
	Czech Republic		Spain		New Zealand		
3.5-11.2%	Lithuania	2.1-7.7%	Poland	17.9-19.2%	United Kingdom	16.3-17.7%	
	Finland		Italy		Korea		Austria
	Greece		Portugal		Switzerland		Spain
	Portugal		Finland		Sweden		Belgium
	Slovenia		Czech Republic		Austria		Finland
	Italy		Lithuania		Spain		Netherlands
	Latvia		Ireland		Denmark		Poland
	Netherlands		Denmark		United States		
	Denmark		Germany		Greece		
11.5-16.8%	Spain	7.9-15.1%	Norway	19.3-20.1%	Slovakia	17.8-20.1%	
	France		Netherlands		Belgium		Slovak Republic
	Estonia		United Kingdom		Lithuania		Greece
	United Kingdom		Sweden		Czech Republic		Slovenia
	Belgium		Slovenia		France		United Kingdom
	United States		Belgium		Portugal		Estonia
	Norway		United States		Netherlands		Denmark
	Germany		Austria		Canada		
	Ireland		France		Estonia		
18.2-41.3%	Austria	16.3-32.7%	Switzerland	20.3-21.4%	Latvia	20.3-24.8%	
	Sweden		New Zealand		Italy		Norway
	Canada		Canada		Germany		Germany
	New Zealand		Luxembourg		Poland		Lithuania
	Israel		Estonia		Japan		Latvia
	Australia		Latvia		Hungary		Hungary
	Switzerland		Australia		Finland		
	Luxembourg		Israel		Slovenia		

Note: Foreign-born population and native-born with at least one foreign-born parent: 2017 or most recent year; 55-64 year-old population: 2015; population of people with disabilities: 2012/2013. People with disabilities are those survey respondents who self-identify as facing barriers to participation in social, economic and daily life associated with a long-standing health problem and/or a basic activity difficulty.
Source: OECD/EU (2018[6]), Settling In 2018: Indicators of Immigrant Integration; UNDESA; Eurostat European Health and Social Integration Survey (EHSIS).

However, these four broad groups mask within-group diversity, which is an aspect worth considering particularly for migrants given the large number of different origin countries. Table 1.2 shows this heterogeneity by classifying OECD countries according to diversity in country of birth, including both the native-born and foreign-born population. The diversity index is calculated as a Herfindahl-Hirschman Index – one of the most common indicators used to measure population diversity – and describes the likelihood that two persons who are randomly drawn from one country are born in the same country. The index ranges from 0 (all persons are born in the same country) to 10 (everyone is born in a different country). This implies that the index not only takes into account the number of countries of birth, but also the size of different groups. To illustrate, when comparing two hypothetical countries where people only come from country A or B, a country where 50% were born in A and 50% in B is ranked as more diverse than a country where the share is, for example, 80% and 20%. Therefore, the index largely mirrors the share of immigrant populations in Table 1.1; countries such as Poland, the Slovak Republic or Mexico score low on the index because their foreign-born population is comparatively small whereas countries with large immigrant populations, such as Luxembourg, Israel and Australia, score high. In most countries, population diversity based on country of birth has increased between 2000 and 2015, notably in Luxembourg, Spain and Norway, and decreased in only a few countries.

Table 1.2. Diversity index based on country of birth, 2015

Low		Moderately low		Moderately high		High	
POL	0.1	PRT	1.3	LVA	2.3	IRL	3.1
SVK	0.2	ITA	1.8	GBR	2.6	SWE	3.2
MEX	0.3	SVN	1.9	NOR	2.7	AUT	3.5
CHL	0.7	NLD	2.1	USA	2.8	CAN	4.5
CZE	0.7	DNK	2.1	EST	2.8	CHE	5.3
HUN	0.8	FRA	2.2	GER	2.8	AUS	5.5
GRC	1.2	ESP	2.2	BEL	2.9	ISR	6.5
FIN	1.2					LUX	7.1

Note: This includes both foreign-born population groups and the native-born.
Source: OECD Database of Immigrants in OECD Countries (DIOC) 2015.

This picture changes when excluding the native-born and only considering country of birth diversity within the immigrant population. Table 1.3 shows that diversity among immigrants is particularly high in Denmark, the United Kingdom and Canada. In most countries, diversity among immigrants has changed little between 2000 and 2015, except for Poland, the Slovak Republic, the Czech Republic and Ireland, where diversity has increased by 1.5 to 2.5 index points as well as in Mexico, where the index decreased by 3.2 points.

Table 1.3. Diversity index among the foreign-born population, 2015

Low		Moderately low		Moderately high		High	
MEX	4.6	IRL	8.5	FRA	9.4	DEU	9.5
EST	5.5	CHL	8.6	FIN	9.4	BEL	9.5
LVA	6.7	LUX	8.9	ISR	9.4	NLD	9.6
SVK	7.2	POL	9.0	ITA	9.4	SWE	9.6
SVN	7.3	PRT	9.1	CHE	9.4	NOR	9.6
CZE	7.4	USA	9.2	AUS	9.4	CAN	9.7
GRC	7.5	AUT	9.3	ESP	9.4	GBR	9.7
HUN	8.0					DNK	9.8

Note: Only includes foreign-born population groups.
Source: OECD Database of Immigrants in OECD Countries (DIOC) 2015.

However, it should be acknowledged that this indicator only provides a limited picture of population diversity. By being restricted to country of birth, the index does not account for native-born children of immigrants. In addition, the index does not show other dimensions of diversity within this group, such as religion (see Box 1.2) and ethnicity, and also treats migrants from countries that have a closer historical connection, e.g. Sweden and Norway or the Czech Republic and Slovakia, as 'diverse' as migrants born on other continents.

Box 1.2. Religious diversity in OECD countries

Religious diversity is another key component when measuring population diversity. The Pew Research Center has created a global index that ranks countries according to their populations' religious diversity, using a Herfindahl-Hirschman Index. The index ranges from 0 (one religious group that everyone belongs to) to 10 (all religious groups are equally large).

The index considers the population size of eight major groups – Buddhism, Christianity, Hinduism, Islam, Judaism, adherents of folk or traditional religions (e.g. African traditional religions or Native American religions); adherents of other religions (e.g. the Baha'i faith, Sikhism or Taoism) and those who are religiously unaffiliated (people identifying as atheists or agnostics).

This rather broad categorisation is due to data limitations, but it should be noted that it necessarily masks heterogeneity within groups. The United States, for example, would score higher if subgroups of Christians were counted.

Figure 1.1. Religious diversity in OECD countries, 2010

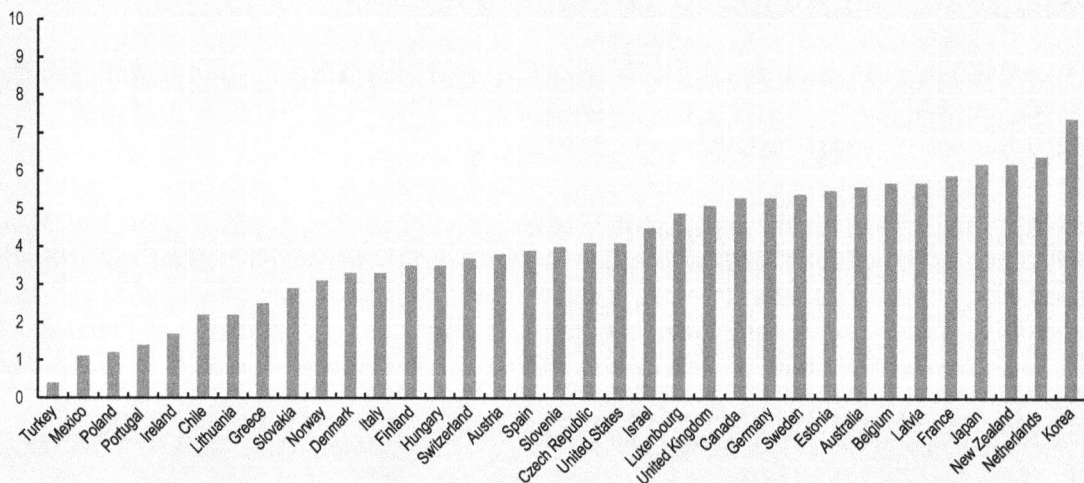

Note: The score ranks countries from 0 to 10. In a country that scores 0, all people belong to the same group, while in a country that scores 10 the eight major groups considered in the study all have the same size.
Source: Pew Research Center, (2014[7]), Global Religious Diversity.
Compared to countries worldwide, religious diversity in OECD countries is rather low. Out of 232 countries and territories covered by the index, 12 countries score above 7 and Korea is the only OECD country in this group. More than one third of OECD countries score above 5. Generally, this is driven by more of the population identifying as unaffiliated to any religious group. All OECD countries with a score above 5 are among the top 10% of countries worldwide with the largest non-religious population groups.

How do OECD countries fare?

Table 1.4. Dashboard on the evolution of gaps and attitudes over the past decade

	Employment gaps				Evolution of employment gaps over past decade			Perceived attitudes			Evolution of attitudes over past decade		
	Gender	Migrant	Age	Disability	Gender	Migrant	Age	Ethnic	LGBTI	Migrants	Ethnic minorities	LGBTI	Migrants
Australia	9.8	3.4	16.6	37.8									
Austria	8.0	8.5	32.8	21.4									
Belgium	8.8	10.2	29.3	31.0									
Canada	5.7	2.6	20.1	26.3									
Chile	19.7	-14.6	9.6										
Czech Republic	14.7	-4.0	24.6	33.5									
Denmark	5.4	10.9	12.7	32.6									
Estonia	6.6	2.8	15.9	23.2									
Finland	3.1	10.8	18.1	22.2									
France	7.1	9.4	29.2	16.2									
Germany	7.4	8.7	14.1	23.0									
Greece	18.3	0.8	29.1	19.0									
Hungary	14.0	-5.6	32.0	26.1									
Iceland	4.8	2.0	6.2	29.8									
Ireland	10.3	0.3	18.3	41.4									
Israel	6.8	-12.4	13.0										
Italy	18.2	-2.3	17.2	15.4									
Japan	15.5	3.6	10.8										
Korea	19.4	-3.2	8.9										
Latvia	3.5	4.0	19.0										
Lithuania	0.4	0.4	17.3										
Luxembourg	7.4	-6.8	43.8	20.0									
Mexico	34.0	8.9	16.4										
Netherlands	9.1	14.4	17.8	31.7									
New Zealand	9.8	1.0	5.9										
Norway	3.2	7.5	10.5	33.8									
Poland	13.3	-3.5	33.7	28.7									
Portugal	6.3	-7.1	26.3	18.9									
Slovakia	11.7	-2.3	27.0	20.1									
Slovenia	6.7	3.0	43.4	26.0									
Spain	11.1	1.7	20.7	24.5									
Sweden	2.9	13.5	9.8	20.6									
Switzerland	9.1	5.9	14.0	13.7									
Turkey	38.5	5.5	26.7										
United Kingdom	9.1	2.6	19.8	30.5									
United States	10.5	-2.3	16.1	43.7									

Note: The chart compares differences in employment rates of men and women; native-born and foreign-born; and prime-age (25-54) and older workers (55-64). Disability status is defined as self-perceived, long-standing activity limitations. **Employment gaps and perceived attitudes** are shown as colour-coded percentiles. **Evolution over 10 years (**2008 and 2018 for attitudes; 2006/07 and 2016/17 for labour market gaps): "red": more than a 2 percentage points change to the favour of diverse groups, "yellow" between a +2 percentage points change and a -2 percentage points change, "red": more than a 2 percentage points change to the detriment of diverse groups (regardless of statistical significance). The evolution refers to differences vis-à-vis the respective comparison group and not absolute values. "Grey": data are not available.
Source: OECD Gender Portal; OECD/EU Settling In: Indicators of Immigrant Integration 2018; OECD Employment Outlook 2018; OECD Connecting People with Jobs 2014; World Gallup Poll.

The "dashboard" in Table 1.4 shows the employment gaps of diverse groups and attitudes towards them, as well as their evolution over a ten-year period.

Labour market inclusion

Employment gaps between men and women, native-born and immigrants, prime age and older workers and people with and without disabilities remain considerable in many OECD countries. Table 1.4 shows these gaps and their evolution over time. However, this should not be interpreted as an indication of how effective diversity policies are in a given country. For example, in countries with large shares of (highly skilled) labour migrants who arrive at the country with a job offer, employment gaps are likely to be smaller than in countries with high shares of family migrants or refugees – two groups that tend to struggle to find a foothold in the labour market (Dumont et al, 2016). Furthermore, it should be noted that fully closing the gaps for older people and people with disabilities is neither realistic, nor desirable, given the health concerns that may prevent individuals in these groups from working.

With these caveats in mind, Table 1.4 shows that both for women and older workers, employment gaps decreased markedly in the majority of OECD countries. Between 2007 and 2017, the gender employment gap decreased by at least 25% in two out of three OECD countries. In three countries, it was more than halved (Luxembourg, Latvia and Lithuania). Nevertheless, on average in the OECD, the employment gap between men and women still stood at 15 percentage points in 2017. In addition, in most countries with large gender gaps, e.g. Turkey, Mexico and Korea, the decline was considerably slower; gaps only decreased by around 10% in the past 10 years. A notable exception is Chile where gender gaps decreased by more than one-third.

As for the gender employment gap, the gap between older and prime age workers has decreased by at least 25% in two out of three OECD countries. Gaps decreased particularly strongly in the Netherlands, Germany, Denmark and Italy by more than 50%. Iceland was the only country where gaps widened, however this increase was small and Iceland remains the OECD country with the smallest employment gap between older and prime-age workers. Nevertheless, gaps remain large at an average 17 pp across OECD countries, ranging from under 10 pp in New Zealand, Korea, Chile and Sweden, to more than 30pp in Belgium, Hungary, Austria, Poland, Slovenia and Luxembourg.

For immigrants, the picture is more mixed. In contrast to women and older people, immigrants have higher employment rates than the native-born in 11 OECD countries. In the majority of these countries, the employment rates of migrant women are higher than among native-born women. In all OECD countries, however, migrant women have lower employment rates than migrant men.. Across the OECD, in 2016/2017, the migrant employment gap was -0.8 pp – meaning that, on average, the employment rates for immigrants were almost 1pp higher. However, this is largely driven by non-EU OECD countries. In the EU, on average, there is a 3.5 pp difference, and in five EU countries (Belgium, Finland, Denmark, Sweden and the Netherlands) the gap is above 10 pp.

For a number of countries where foreign-born are already more likely to work, these gaps have further increased between 2006/07 and 2016/17, most notably in Chile, Israel and Portugal.

Among those countries where gaps have decreased by more than 50%, there are a number of countries where migrants used to have higher employment rates, but are now very close to the native-born rates, e.g. in Ireland, Lithuania and Greece. In some others, such as Spain and Estonia, migrants had slightly lower employment rates than natives in 2016/2017. In Italy, the gap has decreased but migrants still have higher employment rates than natives. Poland is the only country in this group where migrants were less likely to work in 2006/2017, but now have higher employment rates than the native-born (3.5pp). In New Zealand, the employment gap decreased from 6.5 to 1pp and in the United Kingdom from 5.5 to 2.5 pp.

Yet, in countries where migrants continue to have considerably lower employment gaps than natives, relatively little progress was made over the past ten years. In Mexico, France and Finland these gaps widened by around 2pp, while in other countries they have only decreased slightly.

While there are no data available using the same definition of disabilities, gaps are clearly the largest for this group; in 2012, for the 27 OECD countries with available data, the gap was only below 20pp in Italy, France, Switzerland and Germany, while exceeding 30pp in almost one third of countries.

Overall, this dashboard shows that employment gaps have remained substantial in most countries, particularly for older workers and people with disabilities. Iceland is the only OECD country where gaps are below 5% for three groups. For two groups, the gap is below 5% only in Lithuania and Latvia. While employment rates of LGB people cannot be compared over time and data are only available for a few countries,[1] at first glance evidence indicates that gay men are less likely to be employed than heterosexual men, while the reverse occurs when lesbian women are compared with heterosexual women (Valfort, 2017[1]). However, these data, based on household surveys, identify LGB people indirectly, based on the gender of the respondent's partner, thereby limiting the sample to LGB respondents who live in same-sex couples. Looking at same-sex households only is likely to overstate the impact of sexual orientation on employment rates. It does not take into consideration that in heterosexual households, women are less likely to work and also more likely to raise children and take care of domestic tasks than their male partners, whereas in same-sex households these heteronormative forms of division of labour hardly exist (ibid).

Survey data with a sufficiently large sample of homosexual and heterosexual singles is sparse, yet confirms this 'household bias'. In the United Kingdom, for instance, partnered lesbian women are 27% points more likely to work than partnered heterosexual women, whereas single lesbian women are 9% less likely to be employed than heterosexual single women (Aksoy, Carpenter and Frank, 2016[8]).

Attitudes towards diversity, gender equality and diversity policies

Attitudes towards gender equality and openness towards minorities are an important component in assessing how OECD countries are faring and whether public opinion is supportive of strengthening diversity in the workplace.

In the context of overall acceptance of diversity, previous OECD work has shown that openness towards migrants, acceptance of homosexuality and support for gender equality are linked with each other (Valfort, 2017[1]). There is a positive relationship between acceptance of homosexuality and support for gender equality, possibly because homophobia is also linked with supporting traditional gender roles. In addition, in countries where acceptance of homosexuality is higher, the share of people agreeing that native-born should be favoured over migrants when jobs are scarce is lower. This may indicate that fostering openness towards one group may also positively affect attitudes towards other groups.

On the particular issue of immigration, research has shown that in a number of European countries, such as Germany, Norway, Portugal and Spain, attitudes have become more favourable towards migrants over the past decade while in several others, such as Italy and Hungary, it has become more negative (Heath, Richards and Liebig 2018). That is, there was increasing polarisation between European countries in their attitudes. In addition to the growing divergence between countries, there were also a number of countries where internal polarisation occurred, with increasing numbers both of supporters of immigration and of opponents. Attitudes towards gender equality and LGBT people, however, have become steadily more positive over the past decade in the large majority of OECD countries (OECD 2019; OECD 2017).

However, assessing people's attitudes towards diversity and gender equality by the means of opinion polls can lead to biased results. Particularly with socially sensitive topics or when a certain level of consensus has been reached, e.g. around gender equality, respondents are likely to provide an answer they think is expected from them, rather than their 'true' feelings towards an issue. This 'social desirability bias' can therefore distort the measurement of attitudes and provide an overly positive picture of attitudes towards diversity. In addition, positive attitudes may not necessarily be in line with actual behaviour. Therefore, rather than relying on estimates of personal, self-assessed attitudes, the following uses an indicator of how people assess their *neighbourhood's* overall acceptance of diversity, rather than their personal one.

Generally, only a small majority of people in the OECD (55%) believe their neighbourhoods are good places to live for ethnic minorities, LGBT people and immigrants (Figure 1.2). Between 2008 and 2018, the share of respondents agreeing with this statement has increased in most OECD countries, yet at a very uneven pace across countries. In addition, in a number of countries shares had decreased considerably by in 2018 and in more than one-third of OECD countries, at least half of the population does not think that their neighbourhoods are good places for minorities to live. Looking at how people assess the quality of live for different groups shows that in very few countries the share of people thinking that their neighbourhoods are good places to live for LGBT people has decreased. For ethnic and racial minorities this is somewhat more likely to be the case, yet the decrease is most pronounced for immigrants; in almost half of OECD countries the share of people thinking that their neighbourhoods are good places for immigrants to live has decreased.

Figure 1.2. Only a small majority in the OECD agrees that their city or area are good places to live for minorities

Indicator measuring a community's acceptance towards diversity, 2008 and 2018 (or nearest year), share of respondents agreeing with all three questions on diverse groups

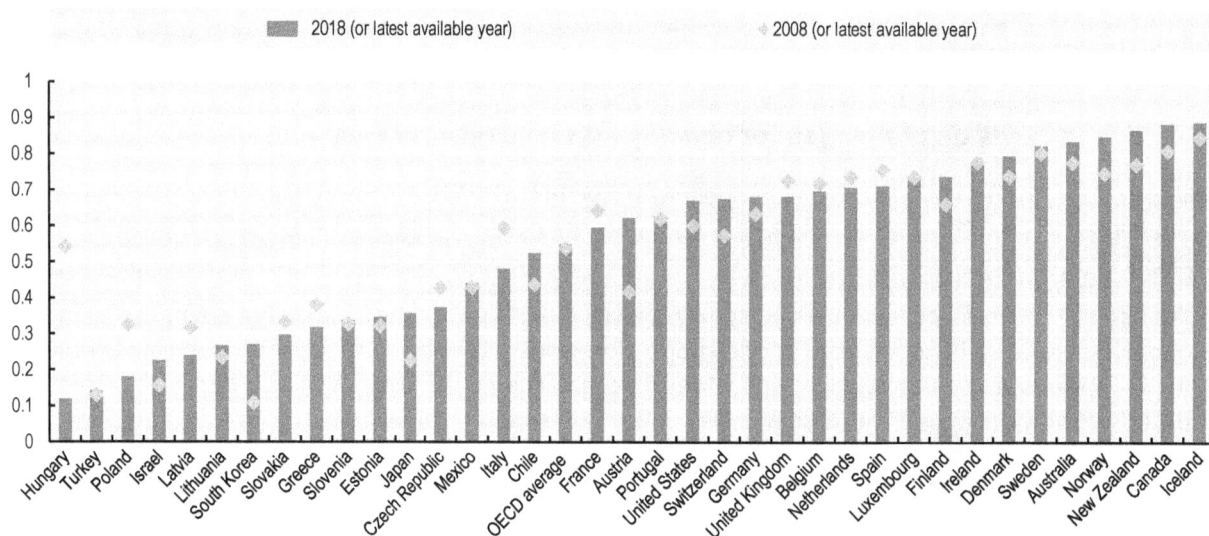

Note: The indicator is composed of three questions: "Is the city or area where you live a good place to live for i) racial and ethnic minorities, ii) gay or lesbian people; iii) immigrants from other countries?".
Source: Gallup World Poll.

However, this indicator measures the perceptions of all residents, whereas the experiences of groups at risk of discrimination may be markedly different. For example, women have a different perception on gender-based discrimination than men. In 2015, on average in the EU, around one in three people agree that gender-based discrimination is fairly or very widespread, but in every EU country, women are more likely to hold this view than men (Eurobarometer, 2015[3]). Differences in perception are particularly large (more than 10 pp) in Estonia, Greece, Finland, France, Sweden and Slovenia.

Survey research among immigrants, their children and ethnic minorities in the EU show that almost one in four respondents felt discriminated against in the 12 months prior to the survey due to their ethnic or immigrant background (European Union Agency for Fundamental Rights, 2017[9]). Feelings of discrimination are most frequent in the area of employment; 12% report being discriminated while looking for work and 9% felt discriminated against at work. Levels are particularly high among respondents from North Africa (15% when looking for work and 14% at work) and for Roma respondents (16% and 5%, respectively). In addition, countries where a large share of the population thinks their community is a good place for minorities to live, e.g. in Finland, the Netherlands and Luxembourg, show some of the highest levels of perceived discrimination.

Experiences of discrimination or fear thereof, particularly at the workplace, also remains a considerable issue for LGBT people. In the EU, around one in three report that they have never disclosed their sexual orientation at work and another 23% state that they have rarely been open about their sexual orientation (European Union Agency for Fundamental Rights, 2014[10]). In addition, country-specific research consistently finds that people with disabilities report high levels of discrimination (see for example Krnjacki et al. (2018[11]) for Australia or Kassam, Williams and Patten (2012[12]) for Canada).

Thus, both the levels of perceived discrimination or fear thereof as well as relatively small changes in how people assess the openness of their neighbourhoods towards diverse groups indicate that although attitudes are slowly improving for some groups, there remains much prejudice.

When looking at the attitudes towards diversity policies in the workplace, a large majority in the EU believes that more should be done. On EU average, only 9% believe that enough is being done to promote diversity in their work place.[2] Another 12% state that this is true to some extent.

At the same time, and somewhat paradoxically, only a minority is supportive of concrete diversity measures in their workplace (Figure 1.3). On average in the EU, only around 36% would support training on diversity issues for employees and employers and 35% would support policies monitoring recruitment to ensure that all candidates with equal skills and qualifications have the same opportunities. Support for monitoring the composition of the workforce is generally lower (32%), and particularly low in Latvia, Estonia and Germany. Only in five countries (Ireland, Sweden, Spain, Portugal and Greece) is the average support for all three measures above 40%.

Figure 1.3. Support for implementing diversity measures in the workplace, 2015

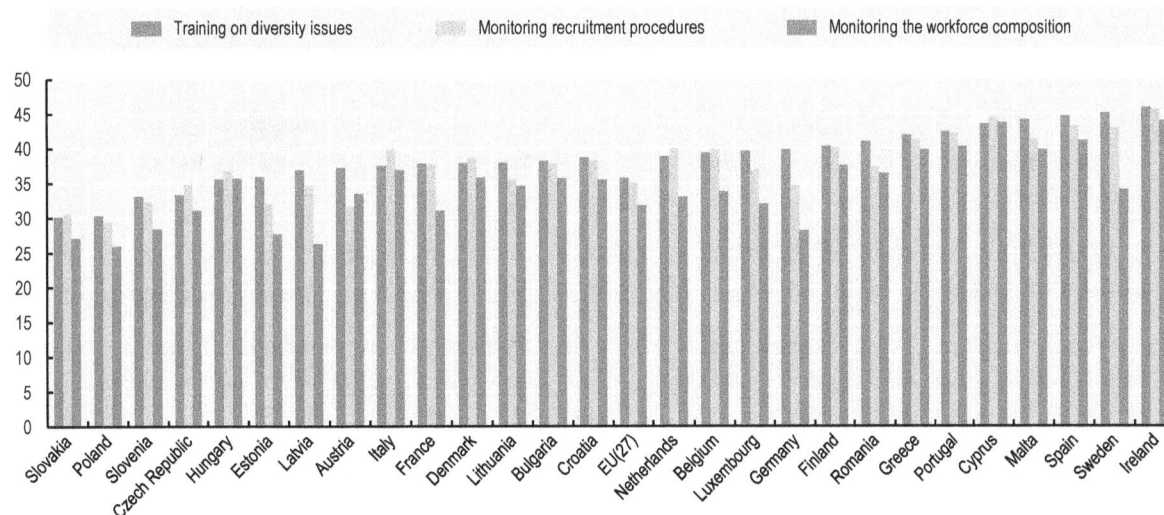

Source: Eurobarometer 2015.

These seemingly contradictory findings – thinking that more needs to be done in the workplace, yet not supporting concrete diversity policies – shows that more abstract support for diversity and equality of opportunity may not necessarily translate into support for diversity policies, possibly reflecting fears that such measures may affect themselves negatively somehow.

References

Aksoy, C., C. Carpenter and J. Frank (2016), "Sexual orientation and earnings: new evidence from the UK", European Bank for Reconstructing and Development Working Paper No. 196. [8]

Balestra, C. and L. Fleischer (2018), "Diversity statistics in the OECD: How do OECD countries collect data on ethnic, racial and indigenous identity?", *OECD Statistics Working Papers*, No. 2018/09, OECD Publishing, Paris, https://dx.doi.org/10.1787/89bae654-en. [2]

Bureau, U. (2018), *https://www.census.gov/about/our-research/race-ethnicity.html*. [4]

Eurobarometer (2015), *Eurobarometer 83.4: Climate Change, Biodiversity, and Discrimination of Minority Groups, May-June 2015*, European Commission. [3]

European Union Agency for Fundamental Rights (2017), *EU MIDIS II - Second European Union Minorities and Discrimination Survey - Main results*, Publications Office of the European Union, Luxembourg. [9]

European Union Agency for Fundamental Rights, F. (2014), *EU LGBT survey – European Union lesbian, gay, bisexual and transgender survey – Main results*, Publications Office of the European Union, Luxembourg. [10]

Kassam, A., J. Williams and S. Patten (2012), "Perceived Discrimination among People with Self-Reported Emotional, Psychological, or Psychiatric Conditions in a Population-Based Sample of Canadians Reporting a Disability", *The Canadian Journal of Psychiatry*, Vol. 57/2, pp. 102-110. [12]

Krnjacki, L. et al. (2018), "Disability-based discrimination and health: findings from an Australian-based population study", *Australian and New Zealand Journal of Public Health*, Vol. 42/2, pp. 172-174. [11]

Mathews, K. et al. (2017), *2015 National Content Test: Race and Ethnicity Analysis Report*, United States Census Bureau. U.S Department of Commerce. Economics and Statistics Administration. [5]

OECD/EU (2018), *Settling In 2018: Indicators of Immigrant Integration*, OECD Publishing, Paris/European Union, Brussels, https://dx.doi.org/10.1787/9789264307216-en. [6]

Pew Research Center (2014), *Global Religious Diversity. Half of the Most Religiously Diverse Countries are in the Asia-Pacific Region*, http://www.pewresearch.org/wp-content/uploads/sites/7/2014/04/Religious-Diversity-full-report.pdf. [7]

Valfort, M. (2017), "LGBTI in OECD Countries: A Review", *OECD Social, Employment and Migration Working Papers*, No. 198, OECD Publishing, Paris, https://dx.doi.org/10.1787/d5d49711-en. [1]

Notes

[1] Australia, Canada, France, Sweden, United Kingdom and United States.

[2] In the Eurobarometer Survey, diversity includes: Ethnic origin, sexual orientation, being over 55 years old, being under 30 years old, religion or beliefs, disability, gender identity and gender.

2 The impact of diversity: A review of the evidence

This chapter examines the evidence on the economic impact of diversity, which yields a rather complicated picture. Contrary to the often assumed, direct positive impact of diversity on business performance, research shows that at the firm level, the business case for diversity is not particularly strong. However, while the impact of diversity might be small, there is a strong economic argument against discrimination and non-inclusion based on the sizeable cost associated with it. Finally, the chapter notes ethical reasons for fostering a just and equitable labour market alongside the economic argument for diversity.

With increasingly diverse societies, there has been a strong interest in better understanding whether and how diversity affects economic outcomes. Findings of a survey of Human Resource professionals across a range of OECD countries (see Box 2.1 for more detail) also show that participating firms have become increasingly concerned with this topic; around two in three think that the topic of diversity management has become more important in their firm in the past five years.

There is a large, multi-disciplinary interest on the impact of diversity, including the field of management and HR, psychology and economics, including labour economics, trade and the political economy literature. Table 2.1 highlights the main channels proposed in the literature on how diversity could positively or negatively impact outcomes at a firm level or affect societies more broadly.

This chapter reviews studies that analyse the economic impact of diversity on the macro (country), meso (region) and micro (firm or team) levels, as diversity is likely to be relevant on all these levels but through different mechanisms and with different outcomes.[1] In addition, it provides a short overview of the literature on how diversity may 'spill over' and impact social cohesion and preferences for redistribution.

Table 2.1. Possible channels of influence of diversity on economic outcomes

Potential positive channels	Potential negative channels
Within firm	
Creativity and innovative thinking: teams with diverse backgrounds, experiences and ideas	**Lower productivity**: e.g. due to communication difficulties
Positive self-selection: unobservable characteristics such as grit and determination to overcome additional hurdles, e.g. labour market discrimination; positive selection of who migrates	**More intra-group conflict**: e.g. due differences in worldviews, discrimination
Trade facilitation and new markets: easier access to markets abroad, better understanding of diverse customer base, new clients	
'Spillovers'	
Increased availability of goods and services: e.g. catering to needs and consumption patterns of diverse clients	**Lower preferences for redistribution**: e.g. taxation, investments in public goods
Increased social cohesion: through stronger labour market inclusion and interactions at the workplace	**Reduced trust and social interactions**: e.g. perceptions of whether others can be generally trusted

Source: Based on (Ozgen, 2018[1]).

Most studies discussed in this section discuss the impact of migrant diversity and gender, which reflects both the interest of the public debate as well as the focus of the literature. Where possible, other forms of diversity (notably age and educational background) are also included. The majority of these studies has focused on Western European and North American countries and looks at the micro level impact, i.e. on the level of firms, teams and executive boards.

Caveats when quantifying diversity and its impacts

Measuring diversity remains a challenge. On the one hand, this is due to data limitations (e.g. on ethnic diversity, see also Balestra and Fleischer (2018[2])), on the other hand, quantifying diversity is not an easy endeavour given the multiple groups any person belongs to (gender, ethnicity, age, religion etc.). Therefore, economic models of cultural diversity mostly focus on only one dimension.

Furthermore, assessing the economic impact is difficult for two main reasons. First, the potential impact of unobserved heterogeneity that may simultaneously influence the outcome variable and ethnic diversity at regional or firm levels is likely to bias the estimated effect sizes of diversity. Panel data fixed effects models, which often help accounting for unobserved heterogeneity, do not work for firm-level studies due to the small within-firm variation. Second, research that can identify causal links between diversity and economic outcomes, e.g. through instrumental variables (IV) estimation, is limited.

Box 2.1. The OECD-Dauphine University HR Survey

The OECD, together with the Paris Dauphine University and with the support of national HR Associations, conducted an online survey in 2017/18 to gather evidence on the experiences and views of HR professionals regarding diversity practices in their firms. The supporting HR Associations included the Australian HR Institute (AHRI), Chartered Professionals in Human Resources (CPHR, Canada) and Human Resources Professionals Association (HRPA, Canada), Association Nationale des DRH (ANDRH, France), Deutsche Gesellschaft für Personalführung (DGFP, Germany), Associazione Italiana per la Direzione del Personale (AIDP, Italy), HR Norge (Norway), Associação Portuguesa de Gestão das Pessoas (APG, Portugal) and Fundación para el Desarrollo de la Función de Recursos Humanos Fundipe (Spain).

The survey was shared by the country's main national HR Association and in total around 2 400 HR professionals in eight OECD countries (Australia, Canada, France, Germany, Italy, Norway, Portugal and Spain) participated. Around 50% of respondents were from Canada, whereas the number of respondents was around 400 for Australia and between 100 and 150 for European OECD countries.

The survey asked whether companies had introduced diversity measures, and if so, what kind of approaches they had chosen and which groups they were targeting. In addition, respondents were asked about the motivation behind these policies, whether outcomes where monitored and evaluated, and what kind of obstacles they had experienced. Lastly, the survey included questions on what kind of support they would like to receive for implementing diversity policies in their firms and what areas of diversity policies should receive more attention in the future.

Considering that the survey was only sent to members of the respective HR Associations and that response rates were low overall, the findings do not provide a representative picture of HR managers or company practices in a given country. Survey findings should be interpreted as giving a first indication of how HR professionals who are likely to be rather open towards diversity view these issues. However, it is clear that more research in this field is needed given the current absence of representative, cross-national data.

The impact of diversity on innovation

Most studies consider either how the shares of foreign graduate students/inventors impact innovation in a given field or they construct a fractionalisation index based on country of birth or nationality, that gives an indication of the workforce's diversity overall.[2] Studies mostly consider patent applications or patents per capita as a proxy for innovation. Table 2.2 provides a snapshot of the studies discussed in the following.

One study on the country-level impact is provided by Chellaraj, Maskus and Mattoo (2008[3]), analysing the impact of the share of foreign graduate students on patent applications, patent grants and non-university patent grants in the United States from 1963-2001. They find a positive impact in the order of 4.5 percent, 6.8 percent and 5.0 percent, respectively for a 10 percent increase in the foreign graduate students as a percentage of total graduate students. Another study confirms a positive impact of foreign-born college graduates, post-college degree holders, and scientists and engineers in the United States. Particularly the last group is found to boost innovation considerably (Hunt and Gauthier-Loiselle, 2010[4]). At the level of US States, they estimate that a 1-percentage point increase in the share of foreign-born STEM college graduates in the overall graduate population boosts patents per capita by 9-18 percent.

In Europe, research has also found a positive relationship between innovation and the share of the foreign-born population on a regional level (Ozgen, Nijkamp and Poot, 2012[5]). In addition, the composition of migrants in terms of different countries of origin is found to be a more important driver for innovation than the regional population size of foreign-born. Another study including around 200 European regions suggests that the impact of migrant diversity on innovation is positive and shows an inverse U-shape relationship. This suggests that there may be an 'optimal level' of migrant diversity when it comes to innovation (Dohse and Gold, 2014[6]).

For Italy, however, one study has found a negative effect of migrant diversity. After distinguishing between low and high-skilled workers, the authors find a negative impact of low-skilled workers on patents; a 1-percentage point increase of low skilled immigrants leads to 0.2 percent decrease in innovation (Bratti and Conti, 2014[7]). For high-skilled migrant workers, their findings are not significant. They argue that this may reflect that immigrants' skills and education often remains underutilised in the Italian labour market. For other countries, however, there is evidence that benefits of diversity for innovation are more apparent in sectors employing relatively more skilled immigrants (see for example Ozgen C, Nijkamp P and Poot (2013[8]) for the Netherlands and Brunow and Stockinger (2013[9]) for Germany).

Relatively few studies look at different elements of diversity. Research by McGuirk and Jordan (2012[10]) is a notable exception, exploring the link between innovation and diversity of educational background, migrant diversity and age diversity in Ireland. They find that diversity in education and nationality have a positive impact on product innovation for a firm. For process innovation, only diversity in nationality has a significant, negative impact. Age diversity is not found to have a significant impact.

Different results are found for Denmark, where age diversity is associated with a negative effect on innovation, which is defined as the introduction of a new product or service (Østergaard, Timmermans and Kristinsson, 2011[11]). More diversity in education and gender appears to boost innovation while the impact of migrant diversity is not significant. Parrotta, Pozzoli and Pytlikova (2014[12]) find for Denmark that diversity in educational background has no impact on patent applications, whereas diversity in country of origin among employees has a positive impact.

Table 2.2. Stylised findings on diversity and innovation

Country	Study	Diversity measure	Outcome measure and effect
United States	Chellaraj et al. (2008)	Foreign-born graduate students	Patent applications (+); Patent grant (+); Non-university patent grants (+)
	Hunt and Gautier-Loiselle (2010)	Foreign-born STEM graduates	Patent per capita (+)
12 western European countries (170 regions)	Ozgen et al. (2012)	Diversity in nationality	Patent applications (+)
EU27 (200 regions)	Dohse and Gold (2014)	Diversity in nationality	Patent applications (+)
ITA (103 regions)	Bratti and Conti (2014)	Diversity in nationality	Patent applications (-)
IRE (app. 1000 firms in 26 counties)	McGuirk and Jordan (2012)		Product innovation & process innovation (+) & (-)
		Diversity in nationality	(+) & (/)
		Diversity in education	(/) & (/)
		Diversity in age	
DEN (1648 Danish firms)	Østergaard et al. (2011)		Introduction of a new product or service: (/)
		Diversity in country of birth	
		Diversity in education	(+)
		Diversity in age	(/)
		More balanced gender composition	(+)
GER (12 000 firms)	Brunow and Stockinger (2013)	Diversity in country of birth	High-skilled (+)
			Low-skilled (/)
DEN (12 000 firms)	Parrotta et al. (2014)		Patent applications
		Diversity in education	(/)
		Diversity in country of birth	(+)

Note: (+) = impact is positive and statistically significant; (-) = impact is negative and statistically significant; (/) = impact is statistically insignificant.
Source: Based on Ozgen (2018).

The impact of diversity on firm performance

Research on firm performance has assessed how diversity in executive boards affects profitability, how performance within teams may change and how higher diversity within firms influences productivity and wages. Much of this literature therefore tests the underlying assumption that more diverse companies can make better decisions and products because women and minorities differ in their knowledge, experiences or management styles and therefore can bring new insights and perspectives.

Diversity in executive boards and its impact on profitability

Table 2.3 shows that most studies on board diversity suggest that the relation between board diversity and performance is not significant or only very weakly positive (for meta-studies on gender board diversity, see Post and Byron (2015[13]) and Pletzer et al. (2015[14]). For example, Post and Byron (2015[13]) assessed 140 studies in a meta-study and found that on average, having more female directors is positively related to returns on assets and returns on equity, but that the effect was very small. The average correlation was .05, i.e. gender board diversity explained around two-tenths of the 1% variance in company performance, while on other indicators, such as stock performance and shareholder returns, the effect was not statistically significant. Studies that have assessed the impact of changes in legislation, e.g. by looking at the impact of newly introduced gender quotas for boards, also tend to find that a subsequently higher share of women does not have a significant effect on firm performance (see for example Ferrari et al. (2016[15]) for Italy.

On the contrary, Adams and Ferreira (2009[16]) found that female directors had a significant effect on board inputs and firm outcomes in a sample of US firms. Female directors appear to have better attendance records than male directors and the attendance of male directors improves following the entry of female members in the board of directors. Furthermore, gender-diverse boards allocate more effort to monitoring, while CEO compensation is found to be more sensitive to stock performance. On average, however, more gender equal boards have a negative effect on corporate performance. The authors argue that this may be linked to too much board monitoring. They find that more gender equal boards have a beneficial effect in companies where shareholder rights are weak and more monitoring is thus beneficial, while the impact is negative for companies with strong shareholder rights. This shows that the relationship between more gender balanced boards and firm performance are complex and may impact different areas of performance differently.

Overall, however, the literature does not allow to make a strong business case; neither for nor against increasing the share of women in company boards. Carter et al. (2010[17]) present similar results for the impact of ethnic diversity in boards in the United States, which is found to have no significant impact on firm performance.

Why this is the case is difficult to determine. There is some evidence suggesting that a positive impact of more gender equal boards is stronger in countries where gender equality is generally higher (Post and Byron, 2015[13]). This can be seen as an indication that board diversity is more than a 'numbers game', but that the context and gender stereotypes matter, for example whether women or minorities on boards have a *de facto* equal standing when it comes to decision making. If they do not, and are there as a token gesture or simply to comply, perhaps reluctantly, with legislation, then their presence on a board is likely to have little impact. Moreover, much of the literature rests on the assumption that more diverse boards can make better decisions because women and minorities differ in their knowledge, experiences or management styles and therefore can bring new insights and perspectives. Particularly for board positions, however, members may be diverse on aspects such as gender or ethnicity, but in other aspects such as educational background, values or professional experiences they might be very similar, hence not always adding much in terms of new perspectives or novel ideas.

Table 2.3. Stylised findings on diverse executive boards and firm performance

Country	Study	Diversity measure	Outcome measure and effect
Meta-analysis of 140 studies in 35 countries (including non-OECD)	Post and Byron (2015)	Share of female directors in boards	Returns on assets (+) Returns on equity (+) Market performance (/)
Meta-analysis of 20 studies in 16 countries (including non-OECD)	Pletzer et al. (2015)	Share of female directors in boards	Ratio of the firm's market value to its book value (Tobin's Q) (/) Returns on assets (/) Returns to equity (/)
US (2000 firms)	Adams and Ferreira (2009)	Share of female directors in boards	Ratio of the firm's market value to its book value (Tobin's Q) (-) Returns to assets (-) Attendance (+)
US (650 firms)	Carter et al. (2010)	Share of female directors and ethnic minority directors on boards	Return on assets (/) Ratio of the firm's market value to its book value (Tobin's Q) (/)

Note: (+) = impact is positive and statistically significant; (-) = impact is negative and statistically significant; (/) = impact is statistically insignificant.
Source: Based on Ozgen (2018).

Diversity, firm productivity and team performance

Studies on how diversity affects productivity at the firm-level, using representative data are rare. Trax, Brunow and Suedekum (2015[18]) show for Germany that migrant diversity has a positive impact on firm productivity, particularly strongly within larger manufacturing plants and less so in service establishments, while the share of migrants, either at the firm level or in the region, has no effect. A similar study for Denmark finds small negative effects on productivity while gender and age are not found to have an impact (Parrotta, Pozzoli and Pytlikova, 2014[12]).

Much of the literature on team performance and diversity belongs to the field of social psychology and management studies and assesses how diverse teams operate at the firm level. Most of the studies are survey-based and usually focus only on specific, usually large firms. This means that findings are not representative of all sectors or even firms within that sector. However, given the breadth of studies in this area, findings can be interpreted as giving an indication on the impact of diversity on team performance.

A number of studies make a difference between 'highly job-related diversity', such as educational background, job position or function in the company, and diversity aspects that are 'less job-related', e.g. gender, ethnicity or age. Measurement of team performance includes multiple indicators, such as efficiency, creativity, innovation and productivity.

Findings are somewhat mixed, but impacts of gender, ethnicity or age diversity are found to be either very small or insignificant. Some meta-analyses find no significant impact of gender composition, ethnicity or age on team performance (Horwitz and Horwitz, 2007[19]; Schneid et al., 2016[20]), while others find negative, but very small impacts (Bell et al., 2011[21]; Joshi and Roh, 2009[22])[3]. Most studies do, however, find a positive relationship between team performance and having teams with different professional backgrounds and other task-related characteristics (Bell et al., 2011[21]; Horwitz and Horwitz, 2007[23]; Joshi and Roh, 2009[22]).

Overall, these findings from meta-analyses seem to suggest that team diversity in terms of gender, ethnicity or age do not matter much for team performance. However, there is some evidence that demonstrates the importance of situational settings by examining under what specific conditions diversity dynamics may unfold and how. Joshi and Roh (2009[22]) show in a more fine-grained analysis that contextual factors, such as type of industry and the relative share of women or ethnic minorities in these teams have a moderating impact on team performance. Accounting for these characteristics generally increases the size of the relationship between team performance and diversity and therefore partially explains the mixed results of individual studies. For example, Joshi and Roh (2009[22])find that higher shares of women and ethnic minorities have a small negative impact in majority male or white teams, but a positive impact when teams are more balanced. This may suggest that when women or ethnic minorities are perceived as 'newcomers' rather than 'just another' colleague, more intra-group conflict may arise or minorities may have difficulties in being heard and taken seriously. In addition, Gonzalez and Denisi (2009[24]) show that in different branches of a large US company the 'diversity climate', i.e. whether employees perceive their workplace as open towards diversity, has a positive impact on the branch's performance. For France, there is also evidence that biased managers have a negative impact on how ethnic minorities perform on the job. When assigned to biased managers (measured by their outcomes in implicit association tests) in a French grocery store chain, ethnic minorities were found to be absent more often, spend less time at work, scan items more slowly and take more time between customers. This appears to be linked to biased managers interacting less with minorities, thereby leading minorities to exert less effort (Glover, Pallais and Pariente, 2017[25]).

Thus, organisational practices, diversity management and non-discrimination policies can be important levers to make the most of a diverse workforce. Gaining a better understanding on how contextual factors mediate the impact of diverse teams is therefore an important area for future research, but due to the limited availability of data on such micro-level aspects of team composition and management, these studies will most likely have to focus on individual firms rather than a representative sample.

The macro-economic impact of diversity

Assessing the macro-economic impact of diversity is not straightforward. A priori, there are no strong reasons that population diversity itself would have a macro-economic effect.

Research on how population diversity affects macro-economic outcomes has largely focused on the impact of immigrant diversity and mostly find a positive impact for high-income countries. The majority of country-specific studies focuses on the United States.

A study on 195 countries shows that the diversity of immigrants is positively associated with economic prosperity, particularly so for skilled migrants in high-income countries; a one percentage point increase of the diversity of skilled migrants increases long-run economic output, measured by GDP per capita, by 2% (Alesina, Harnoss and Rapoport, 2016[26]). In addition, there is evidence for the United States that at the city level, diversity generally has no significant impact on wages for low-skilled jobs, but has a positive impact on wages in high-skilled, high-income jobs that demand complex problem-solving (Cooke and Kemeny, 2017[27]). Similarly, panel data on US states over the 1960-2010 period indicates that diversity among highly educated immigrants has positive impact on economic growth, whereas diversity among low-skilled migrants has a no effect (Docquier et al., 2018[28]). Results for Germany show a smaller effect, but similar pattern (Suedekum, Wolf and Blien, 2014[29]).

These findings point in the same direction as the literature focusing on the firm level, as they suggest that diversity is likely to have a stronger positive impact in high-skilled employment. Other studies show similar positive effects on GDP per capita, however effects are found to be stronger in low-income countries (see for example Bove and Elia (2017[30]).

Looking at regions within 12 EU countries,[4] higher immigrant diversity is found to have a positive impact on the productivity and wages of natives. This relationship is even stronger in more densely populated areas, pointing to possible agglomeration effects, i.e. the benefits of firms and people located near to each other (Bellini et al., 2008[31]). Similar results are found for US cities (Ottaviano and Peri, 2006[32]).

Using historic data from 1870–1920 from the age of mass migration to the United States, Ager and Brückner (2013[33]) find that higher immigrant diversity is related to stronger economic development at the county level, whereas a stronger polarisation, i.e. few, but comparatively larger country of origin groups living in counties with a American-born majority, has the opposite effect.

Diversity, social cohesion and preferences for redistribution

There is a large literature that goes beyond the economic impact of diversity and seeks to assess how ethnic and immigrant diversity affects social cohesion and preferences for redistribution. Most of this literature focusing on OECD countries has addressed how diversity can affect trust, voting patterns, civic participation, preferences for redistribution and investment into public goods. Despite some contradictory findings, evidence generally points to a negative relationship between diversity and these indicators of social cohesion, although findings vary strongly across countries, level of analysis and the inclusion of moderating factors. Generally, the negative impact of ethnic diversity appears to be more pronounced in the United States than in European OECD countries (for an overview, see (Alesina and La Ferrara, 2005[34]; Montalvo and Reynal-Querol, 2014[35]; Dinesen and Sønderskov, 2017[36])).

However, the relationship between diversity and social cohesion is not clear-cut. The literature shows that a number of factors have a strong mediating impact; social exclusion and disadvantage, inequality, inter-group contact and social interactions as well as the role of governance and institutions are important explanatory factors. In other words, what drives an often-observed erosion of social cohesion is not diversity itself, but rather contextual factors related to socio-economic status, inequality and governance. For example, studies on social cohesion in neighbourhoods show that the key element for weak social cohesion is the low socio-economic status of a neighbourhood rather than its ethnic diversity (Letki, 2008[37]; Tolsma, van der Meer and Gesthuizen, 2009[38]; Laurence, 2017[39]). Another area of the literature looks specifically at the impact of inequality between groups on public goods provision and attitudes towards redistribution. On a country level, a study on 46 countries – mostly high-income countries and emerging economies – finds a strong negative relationship between the level of provision of public goods and inequality between ethnic groups measured as differences in mean incomes across groups. In addition, findings suggest that these economic differences actually lead to lower public goods provision, particularly in countries with weaker democratic structures (Baldwin and Huber, 2010[40]). Delhey and Newton (2005[41]) find that generalised social trust is not directly impacted by diversity, whereas it is negatively associated with income inequality.

Regarding attitudes towards social spending and redistribution, in EU countries, positive attitudes among native-born towards income redistribution decrease with higher immigrant diversity and a higher share of immigrants in the population (Alesina, Harnoss and Rapoport, 2014[42]). Overall, however, the effect is small; a 1-percentage point increase in the share of foreign-born lowers support for redistribution only by about 0.2 percent. In addition, this effect is even smaller when immigrants come from high-income countries and when native-born are highly educated. This indicates that attitudes towards redistribution are not primarily influenced by ethnic diversity, but rather by the socio-economic status of migrants and possibly an assumed dependence on social welfare benefits.

Furthermore, there is mounting evidence that social interactions between groups has a positive impact on social cohesion, and particularly, trust. Research on the United States and Canada show that white people living in diverse neighbourhoods are more trusting when they regularly talk to their neighbours (Stolle, Soroka and Johnston, 2008[43]). This highlights not only the role stereotypes play in eroding social cohesion, but also the importance of social interactions to overcome them. This is particularly likely in settings where people encounter each other as equals and as part of a routine or with a common goal, e.g. in the workplace or at school, as such interactions can help reduce anxiety and increase empathy (for an overview, see Pettigrew et al., (2011[44])).

Lastly, how diversity influences social cohesion hinges on the quality of governance structures and institutions. Studies have shown that good governance on a country and regional level increase generalised trust and render an otherwise negative impact of diversity insignificant (Murtin et al., 2018[45]; Delhey and Newton, 2005[41]). Similarly, Kemeny and Cooke (2017[46]) find that in cities with low levels of inclusive institutions, the benefits of diversity are modest or non-existent, whereas in cities with high levels of inclusive institutions, the benefits of immigrant diversity are significant and positive.

The societal and economic cost of non-inclusion

In the context of increasingly diverse populations, there is a clear interest in gauging the economic impact of diversity. The previous sections have shown that overall, the evidence on the economic impact of diversity yields a rather complicated picture. Contrary to the often assumed, direct positive impact of diversity on business performance, research shows that at the firm level, the business case for diversity is not particularly strong.

However, while the impact of diversity might be small, there is a strong economic argument against discrimination and non-inclusion based on the sizeable cost associated with it.

Quite evidently, the economic exclusion or inactivity of large population groups comes at a high cost, particularly against the backdrop of demographic change related to ageing populations and increasing shares of groups that have been traditionally disadvantaged in the labour market, such as people with disabilities, migrants and ethnic minorities. Some studies seek to quantify the cost of continuing non-inclusion of diverse populations. France, for example, could gain around EUR 150 billion, or 6.9% of the 2015 GDP, over 20 years (i.e. a 0.35% increase in GDP per year) from elevating employment rates of women, French-born with a migration background, residents of disadvantaged neighbourhoods and people with disabilities to the average employment level (Bon-Maury et al., 2016[47]). Similarly, if the gender gap in labour force participation across the OECD were to be reduced by 25% by 2025, this could add one percentage point to projected baseline GDP growth across the OECD over the period 2013-25, and almost 2.5 percentage points if gaps were halved (OECD, 2017[48]). While these estimates are not based on a general equilibrium model, i.e. taking into account how this may impact the behaviour of supply, demand and prices in the overall economy, it nevertheless demonstrates that there are substantial macroeconomic gains in increasing labour market inclusion.

Employers will increasingly feel the cost of discriminatory behaviour in the context of growing labour market shortages, as their competitiveness will suffer from irrational hiring preferences (Gary Becker, 1957). Indeed, a field testing study has found that compared to natives, candidates with a foreign sounding name are equally often invited to a job interview if they apply for occupations for which vacancies are difficult to fill (Baert, Cockx and Gheyle, 2015[49]). Similarly, an analysis of reports filed in the context of the Dutch diversity law *Wet SAMEN* finds that skilled labour market shortage impacts ethnic minority representation positively (Verbeek, 2012[50]).

The economic dimension, however, is not the justification upon which efforts to foster diverse workforces ultimately rest. Economic arguments can only serve to reinforce the obligation of ensuring the labour market inclusion of diverse groups rooted in the idea of promoting a society that is just and equitable, valuing diversity, providing equal opportunities to all its members, irrespective of their various characteristics.

Thus, while there might not be a clear-cut business case for diversity, there is a strong social justice obligation, as well as a business case to prevent discrimination and non-inclusion. This rationale is a logical consequence of talent being distributed equally among the population – to make the most of increasingly diverse workforces, businesses and policy makers must ensure that opportunity also is.

References

Adams, R. and D. Ferreira (2009), "Women in the boardroom and their impact on governance and performance", *Journal of financial economics*, Vol. 94, pp. 291-309. [16]

Ager, P. and M. Brückner (2013), "Cultural diversity and economic growth: Evidence from the US during the age of mass migration", *European Economic Review*, Vol. 64, pp. 76-97. [33]

Alesina, A., J. Harnoss and H. Rapoport (2016), "Birthplace diversity and economic prosperity", *Journal of Economic Growth*, Vol. 21, pp. 101-138. [26]

Alesina, A., J. Harnoss and H. Rapoport (2014), "Immigration, Diversity and Attitudes to Redistribution: A European Perspective", *Unpublished manuscript*. [42]

Alesina, A. and E. La Ferrara (2005), *Ethnic Diversity and Economic Performance*. [34]

Baert, S., B. Cockx and N. Gheyle (2015), "Is There Less Discrimination in Occupations Where Recruitment Is Difficult?", *ILR Review*, Vol. 68/3, pp. 467-500, http://dx.doi.org/10.1177/0019793915570873. [49]

Baldwin, K. and J. Huber (2010), "Economic versus Cultural Differences: Forms of Ethnic Diversity and Public Goods Provision", *American Political Science Review*, Vol. 104/4, pp. 644-662. [40]

Balestra, C. and L. Fleischer (2018), "Diversity statistics in the OECD: How do OECD countries collect data on ethnic, racial and indigenous identity?", *OECD Statistics Working Papers*, No. 2018/09, OECD Publishing, Paris, https://dx.doi.org/10.1787/89bae654-en. [2]

Bellini, E. et al. (2008), "Cultural diversity and economic performance: Evidence from European regions", *HWWI Research Papers*, No. 3-14, Hamburg Institute of International Economics (HWWI), Hamburg. [31]

Bell, S. et al. (2011), "Getting Specific about Demographic Diversity Variable and Team Performance Relationships: A Meta-Analysis", *Journal of Management*, Vol. 37/3, pp. 709-743. [21]

Bon-Maury, G. et al. (2016), *Le coût économique des discriminations - Rapport à la ministre du Travail, de l'Emploi, de la Formation professionnelle et du Dialogue social et au ministre de la Ville, de la Jeunesse et des Sports*, France Stratégie, Paris. [47]

Bove, V. and L. Elia (2017), "Migration, Diversity, and Economic Growth", *World Development*, Vol. 89, pp. 227-239. [30]

Bratti, M. and C. Conti (2014), "The effect of (mostly unskilled) immigration on the innovation of Italian regions", IZA Discussion Paper No. 7922. [7]

Brunow, S. and B. Stockinger (2013), "Establishments' and regions' cultural diversity as a source of innovation: Evidence from Germany", NORFACE Discussion Paper, No. 22. [9]

Carter, D. et al. (2010), "The Gender and Ethnic Diversity of US Boards and Board Committees and Firm Financial Performance", *Corporate Governance: An International Review*, Vol. 18/5, pp. 396–414. [17]

Chellaraj, G., K. Maskus and A. Mattoo (2008), "The contribution of international graduate students to US innovation", *Review of International Economics*, Vol. 16, pp. 444-462. [3]

Cooke, A. and T. Kemeny (2017), "Cities, immigrant diversity, and complex problem solving", *Research Policy*, Vol. 46, pp. 1175-1185. [27]

Delhey, J. and K. Newton (2005), "Predicting Cross-National Levels of Social Trust: Global Pattern or Nordic Exceptionalism?", *European Sociological Review*, Vol. 21/4, pp. 311-327. [41]

Dinesen, P. and K. Sønderskov (2017), "Ethnic Diversity and Social Trust: A Critical Review of the Literature and Suggestions for a Research Agenda", in Uslaner, E. (ed.), *The Oxford Handbook of Social and Political Trust*, Oxford University Press, http://oxfordhandbooks.com/view/10.1093/oxfordhb/9780190274801.001.0001/oxfordhb-9780190274801-e-13. [36]

Docquier, F. et al. (2018), "Birthplace Diversity and Economic Growth: Evidence from the Us States in the Post-World War II Period", *IZA Discussion Paper Series*, No. 11802, IZA - Institute of Labor Economics. [28]

Dohse, D. and R. Gold (2014), "Determining the Impact of Cultural Diversity on Regional Economies in Europe", WWW for Europe project WP no 58. [6]

Ferrari, G. et al. (2016), "Gender Quotas: Challenging the Boards, Performance, and the Stock Market", *IZA Discussion Paper*, No. No.10239, Institute for the Study of Labor. [15]

Glover, D., A. Pallais and W. Pariente (2017), "Discrimination as a self-fulfilling prophecy: evidence from French grocery stores", *The Quarterly Journal of Economics*, pp. 1219-1260. [25]

Gonzalez, J. and A. Denisi (2009), "Cross-level effects of demography and diversity climate on organizational attachment and firm effectiveness", *Journal of Organizational Behavior*, Vol. 30, pp. 21-40. [24]

Horwitz, S. and I. Horwitz (2007), "The Effects of Team Diversity on Team Outcomes: A Meta-Analytic Review of Team Demography", *Journal of Management*, Vol. 33/6, pp. 987-1015. [19]

Horwitz, S. and I. Horwitz (2007), "The Effects of Team Diversity on Team Outcomes: A Meta-Analytic Review of Team Demography", *Journal of Management*, Vol. 33/6, pp. 987-1015. [23]

Hunt, J. and M. Gauthier-Loiselle (2010), "How much does immigration boost innovation?", *American Economic Journal: Macroeconomics*, Vol. 2, pp. 31-56. [4]

Joshi, A. and H. Roh (2009), "The role of context in work team diversity research: A meta-analytic review", *Academy of Management Journal*, Vol. 52/3, pp. 559-627. [22]

Kemeny, T. and A. Cooke (2017), "Urban Immigrant Diversity and Inclusive Institutions", *Economic Geography*, Vol. 93/3, pp. 267-291. [46]

Laurence, J. (2017), "Wider-community Segregation and the Effect of Neighbourhood Ethnic Diversity on Social Capital: An Investigation into Intra-Neighbourhood Trust in Great Britain and London", *Sociology*, Vol. 51/5, pp. 1011-1033. [39]

Letki, N. (2008), "Does Diversity Erode Social Cohesion? Social Capital and Race in British Neighbourhoods", *Political Studies*, Vol. 56/1, pp. 99-126. [37]

McGuirk, H. and D. Jordan (2012), "Local labour market diversity and business innovation: evidence from Irish manufacturing businesses", *European Planning Studies*, Vol. 20, pp. 1945-1960. [10]

Montalvo, J. and M. Reynal-Querol (2014), "Cultural Diversity, Conflict, and Economic Development", in Ginsburgh, Victor A. Throsby, D. (ed.), *Handbook of the Economics of Art and Culture*, Elsevier. [35]

Murtin, F. et al. (2018), "Trust and its determinants: Evidence from the Trustlab experiment", *OECD Statistics Working Papers*, No. 2018/02, OECD Publishing, Paris, http://dx.doi.org/10.1787/869ef2ec-en. [45]

OECD (2017), *The Pursuit of Gender Equality. An Uphill Battle*, http://dx.doi.org/10.1787/9789264281318-en (accessed on 5 October 2017). [48]

Østergaard, C., B. Timmermans and K. Kristinsson (2011), "Does a Different View Create Something New? The Effect of Employee Diversity on Innovation", *Research Policy*, Vol. 40, pp. 500–509. [11]

Ottaviano, G. and G. Peri (2006), "The economic value of cultural diversity: evidence from US cities", *Journal of Economic Geography*, Vol. 6, pp. 9-44. [32]

Ozgen C, Nijkamp P and J. Poot (2013), "The Impact of Cultural Diversity on Firm Innovation: Evidence from Dutch micro-data", *IZA Journal of Migration*, Vol. 2/18. [8]

Ozgen, C. (2018), "The economic impact of diversity: A literature review", Background Report for the OECD. [1]

Ozgen, C., P. Nijkamp and J. Poot (2012), "Immigration and innovation in European regions", in Nijkamp, N., J. Poot and M. Sahin (eds.), *Migration Impact Assessment: New Horizons*, Edward Elgar Publishing. [5]

Parrotta, P., D. Pozzoli and M. Pytlikova (2014), "Labor diversity and firm productivity", *European Economic Review*, Vol. 66, pp. 144-179. [12]

Pettigrew, T. et al. (2011), "Recent advances in intergroup contact theory", *International Journal of Intercultural Relations*, Vol. 35, pp. 271-280. [44]

Pletzer, J. et al. (2015), "Does Gender Matter? Females on Corporate Boards and Firm Financial Performance - A Meta-Analysis", *Academy of Management Proceedings*, Vol. 2015/1. [14]

Post, C. and K. Byron (2015), "Women on Boards and Firm Financial Performance: A Meta-Analysis", *Academy of Management Journal*, Vol. 58/5, pp. 1546-1571. [13]

Schneid, M. et al. (2016), "Age diversity and team outcomes: a quantitative review", *Journal of Managerial Psychology*, Vol. 31/1, pp. 2-17. [20]

Stolle, D., S. Soroka and R. Johnston (2008), "When Does Diversity Erode Trust? Neighborhood Diversity, Interpersonal Trust and the Mediating Effect of Social Interactions", *Political Studies*, Vol. 56/1, pp. 57-75. [43]

Suedekum, J., K. Wolf and U. Blien (2014), "Cultural diversity and local labour markets", *Regional Studies*, Vol. 48, pp. 173-191. [29]

Tolsma, J., T. van der Meer and M. Gesthuizen (2009), "The impact of neighbourhood and municipality characteristics on social cohesion in the Netherlands", *Acta Politica*, Vol. 44/3, pp. 286-313.   [38]

Trax, M., S. Brunow and J. Suedekum (2015), "Cultural diversity and plant-level productivity", *Regional Science and Urban Economics*, Vol. 53, pp. 85-96.   [18]

Verbeek, S. (2012), "Do "hard" diversity policies increase ethnic minority representation?: An assessment of their (in)effectiveness using administrative data.", *Personnel Review*, Vol. 41/5, http://dx.doi.org/10.1108/00483481211249157.   [50]

Notes

[1] Parts of this chapter are based on a background report on the economic impact of diversity, provided by Ceren Ozgen (Marie Sklodowska-Curie Fellow at the Department of Economics and the Institute for Research into Superdiversity (IRiS) at the University of Birmingham).

[2] This index accounts both for the heterogeneity of a population as well as the size of different population groups. It measures the probability that two people who are randomly selected from a sample belong to different groups and is the inverse of the Herfindahl-Hirschmann index used in Chapter 3 to build a migrant diversity index.

[3] Most studies considered in these meta-analyses were conducted in the US.

[4] Austria, Belgium, Denmark, France, former Western Germany, Ireland, Italy, the Netherlands, Portugal, Spain, Sweden and the United Kingdom.

3 Diversity policies in the OECD and evidence on their effectiveness

This chapter assesses OECD countries' existing policies for diversity in the labour market in light of the gradually growing body of literature evaluating their impact. It considers the role of non-discrimination legislation, as well as the effects of hiring quotas, financial incentives and awards for firms that hire a diverse workforce. Furthermore, it evaluates diversity instruments such as anonymous job applications, outreach to underrepresented groups and diversity trainings for staff.

This chapter assesses OECD countries' existing policies for diversity in the labour market in light of the gradually growing body of literature evaluating the impact of such instruments. The effort to synthesise diversity instruments with the evidence in a comparative, cross-country manner must be preceded by a note of caution: the evidence currently at hand is still sparse and highly context-specific. The majority of studies evaluates diversity measures in a particular country, if not a particular firm, with limited transferability of results for a given policy instrument from one context to another.

It is, however, possible to provide initial pointers on how and under which circumstances existing diversity measures seem to promote anti-discrimination and diversity efforts. Taking an evidence-based view on what has been learned in several decades of "diversity and inclusion" on the political agenda of OECD countries, this overview seeks to derive lessons for future policymaking. A key result of this review is that diversity efforts must be targeted to the national context and the situation of a specific diverse group – otherwise, well-intended diversity measures can be ineffective and, at worst, counterproductive.

The chapter is based on a recent policy questionnaire answered by 30 OECD countries, as well as the findings of the OECD-Dauphine University HR survey conducted with around 2 400 HR professionals in eight OECD countries (see Box 3.1). Each section discusses a common policy instrument and its effectiveness.

Non-discrimination legislation and the role of equality bodies

In virtually all OECD countries, diverse populations are protected by non-discrimination legislation in the field of employment. In almost all countries, discrimination is prohibited on the grounds of sex/gender and gender identity, sexual orientation, age and race, ethnic origin or skin colour (see Annex A for an overview of protected grounds in OECD countries). Religion or belief is another commonly protected ground, while some provisions are specific to certain countries, e.g. for indigenous, native or aboriginal people in Canada, the United States and Australia. Australia, France, Finland, the Netherlands and Portugal notably go well beyond the commonly protected groups, including a variety of grounds such as political or trade union activity, criminal history, family or marital status, physical appearance, type of contract or place of domicile. Often, the above are non-exhaustive lists (including e.g. "any other grounds") and eight countries explicitly recognise discrimination on multiple grounds (see Box 3.1).

Box 3.1. Multiple and intersectional discrimination

Legislation in many OECD countries recognises multiple, additive, or cumulative discrimination, i.e. discrimination occurring on the basis of more than one ground. This acknowledges that a person who is, for example, discriminated against on grounds of race might also suffer discrimination on grounds of gender, sexual orientation, religion or belief, age or disability.

A different approach focuses on the *synergies* between particular grounds, and the new forms of discrimination it creates. This phenomenon, first coined in the academic debate by (Crenshaw, 1989[1]), is known as the concept of intersectional discrimination. Proponents of intersectional approaches maintain that the focus on single grounds renders invisible the challenges faced by those at the intersection of grounds. This invisibility, so they argue, is part of a deeper structural problem of anti-discrimination and diversity efforts, namely that the categories on which grounds are based tend to predominantly focus on the barriers faced by the more privileged of the group: white women in the case of gender discrimination, and ethnic minority men in the case of race discrimination. Neither of those categories accurately capture the discrimination experienced by ethnic minority women.

While multiple discrimination can be addressed within existing legal frameworks, the situation with intersectionality is more complicated. Non-discrimination laws, and most diversity polices, cannot possibly

---

cater to specific experiences of discrimination created by any combination of grounds. Intersectionality can, however, be mainstreamed into existing frameworks – pointing out the large diversity of experiences within a given group where necessary, rather than assuming homogeneity. Such an approach could for example inform legal proceedings, to explain in courts that a case made by black women cannot be dismissed just because the employer did hire black people who were men and women who were white. Likewise, anti-bias trainings could illustrate the specific bias against Muslim men that one might not similarly hold against Muslim women (compare Valfort (2015[2])).

Yet, intersectional discrimination remains difficult to monitor and analyse, as existing data mostly do not allow for disaggregation on grounds such as ethnic background or disability. More recently, however, there is increasing guidance on how such intersectional 'equality data' could be collected (Balestra and Fleischer, 2018[3]; Makkonen, 2016[4])

Twelve out of the 30 OECD countries that answered the questionnaire include socio-economic disadvantage as a protected ground in their anti-discrimination legislation. The variety in definitions used, including social origin, social status or social class as well as wealth, income, financial or economic situation, illustrates the difficulty with operationalising socio-economic status (SES). As it targets a changing characteristic, discrimination based on SES is not straightforward to measure and a cut-off is difficult to determine (see Box 3.3).

The empirical literature on the effects of non-discrimination legislation remains scant, with most studies addressing the US context. Existing evidence suggests that the initial adoption of the landmark anti-discrimination law Title VII of the 1964 Civil Rights Act initially aided the economic status of black workers in terms of both employment and wages, but with diminishing returns over time (Donohue, 2005[5]; OECD, 2008[6]).

Other studies highlight possible unintended side-effects of legal protection. In their analysis of disabled workers' employment following the American Disabilities Act (ADA), (Acemoglu and Angrist, 2001[7]) observe a decline in employment of disabled workers after the ADA went into effect. The authors suggest that with the requirements to accommodate the needs of disabled employees, as well as regulations regarding their hiring, firing and pay, the perceived costs of might have led employers to refrain from hiring workers with disabilities. It was not possible to identify the component of the law that caused the effect, which might have been the cost of accommodation of disabled workers (costly equipment etc.) as well as the higher cost of hiring due to fear of litigation. Other studies argue that the decrease in the employment of workers with disabilities during the 1990s was a result of changes that expanded Social Security Disability Insurance (SSDI) eligibility and benefits (Autour and Duggan, 2003).

Aside from effects on employers' behaviour, the mere institutional decision to protect certain groups may impact the wider society's perception of social norms and influence attitudes towards diverse groups. A recent study using experimental strategies investigated how the June 2015 US Supreme Court ruling in favour of same-sex marriage affected behaviour and attitudes towards minority groups (Tankard and Paluck, 2017[8]). The authors observe that attitudes in support of gay marriage were significantly more positive among participants who were told that a positive ruling was the most likely outcome. The subsequent five-wave longitudinal time-series indeed indicated that after the actual ruling, participants believed that social norms shifted in favour of same-sex marriage. These results are in line with previous research suggesting that changes in legal norms, if democratic in nature, are seen as a signal of where the public stands, which in turn can influence attitudes and behaviour (Cialdini and Goldstein, 2004[9]).

However, for non-discrimination legislation to have any effect, awareness of legal provisions is crucial, as are effective recourse mechanisms for individuals who feel discriminated against (Heath, Liebig and Simon, 2013[10]). In almost all OECD countries, specialised equality bodies and ombudsman offices assume this task alongside civil society initiatives, trade unions and NGOs.

The competences of equality bodies in OECD countries vary. Generally, such bodies provide information about non-discrimination laws and the possibility to take legal action. In some countries, including Italy, Mexico, Sweden, the United Kingdom, Belgium and Denmark, equality bodies have litigation powers. However, even when legal representation through an equality body is possible, it is not provided in a systematic way and only strategic cases that can provide clarifications on the law or create precedence are taken up. Another role of equality bodies is that of a third party in mediation and conciliation procedures, an approach that may be less damaging to the employer-employee relationship than litigation. In almost all countries, specialised bodies assume an awareness-raising role, conducting information campaigns and/or trainings related to anti-discrimination issues in their country (see Figure 3.1).

Figure 3.1. Awareness-raising activities conducted by equality bodies in 2017

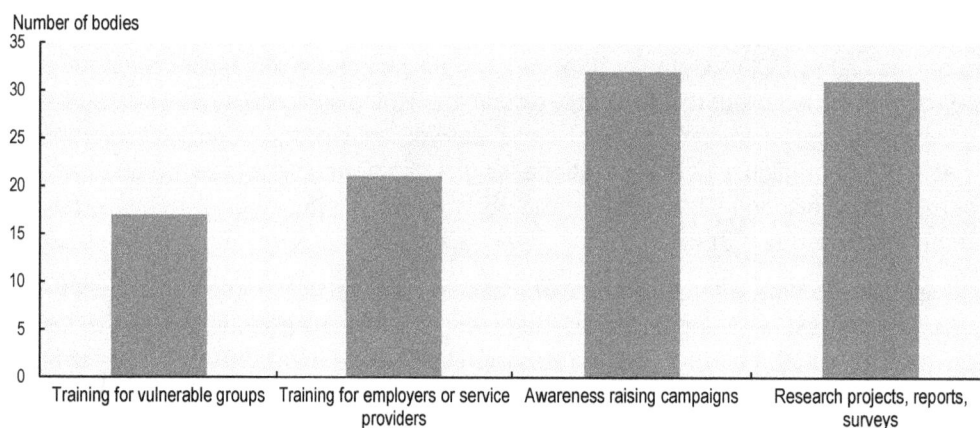

Note: See Annex B for an overview of equality bodies that have responded to the survey.
Source: OECD "Diversity at Work" questionnaire.

Figure 3.2 indicates that in all European OECD countries for which data is available, awareness of non-discrimination provisions has increased between 2007 and 2015. However, the numbers also show that there is still a long way to go in terms of awareness of rights. In the majority of countries, less than half of the population would know their rights if they were to become a victim of discrimination or harassment.

Figure 3.2. Public awareness about legal rights in case of discrimination or harassment

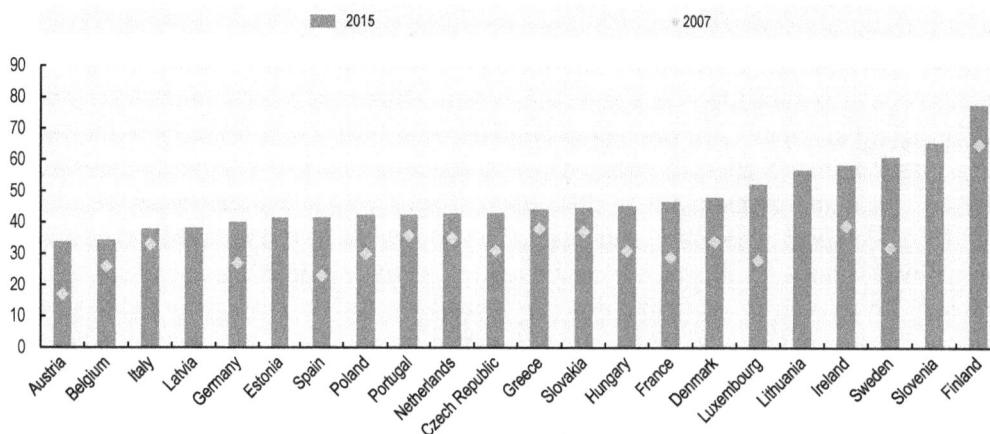

Source: Eurobarometer (2007) and (2015).

Further strengthening the awareness of workplace rights is critical. This must go together with strong recourse mechanisms ensuring that potential victims of discrimination can actually avail themselves of their rights, while being protected from retaliation (see Box 3.2).

Box 3.2. Towards effective and trusted recourse mechanisms to promote diversity

Promoting diversity requires implementing both effective anti-discrimination provisions and accessible and trusted recourse mechanisms to ensure that the rights of diverse groups are protected. OECD countries have put in place a variety of recourse mechanisms to deal with cases of discrimination in the labour market, ranging from ordinary courts, labour courts, quasi-judicial and specialised tribunals, to various alternative dispute resolution (ADR) mechanisms, such as mediation.

Despite a solid common ground in most OECD countries, challenges remain in enforcing the various provisions and enabling different groups of individuals to claim their rights within and outside of courts. Indeed, the data from the World Justice Project shows that many people from the most discriminated groups are most likely to take no action when facing alleged discriminations – as these groups are not always aware of the scope of anti-discrimination legislation, or where and how to find and use available assistance. For example, the 2016 UNDP/UNODC Global Study of Legal Aid showed that in some countries the absence of specialised services for women was a significant obstacle to women's access to legal aid. The study found that women did not always understand how legal aid services can help them and were not confident in the quality of legal support available to them.

In addition, many vulnerable workers tend to face numerous economic, structural, and institutional challenges, which hinder their access to justice, including the complexity and cost of legal processes, time restrictions, and geographical and physical constraints.   Studies also highlight that trust in the justice system and individual recourse mechanisms is also an important factor in determining whether people seek legal assistance, or take any action to resolve their legal problems, including when experiencing unequal treatment.

While ADRs often present an effective alternative to litigation, their use must be accompanied by the appropriate safeguards to avoid that they create additional barriers for people in claiming their rights. In particular, while ADRs are often found more effective in individual discrimination cases, these mechanisms are more limited when dealing with more systemic discrimination and structural causes of group exclusion in employment in specific sectors. This is particularly essential when vulnerable workers are parties to a discrimination case, as ADR can ignore the special needs of vulnerable parties by searching for an agreement. More broadly, there is often little communication of the available recourse mechanisms and limited evidence of the extent to which they meet the need for protecting employment rights.

In order to effectively support the development of culture of diversity where all individuals are empowered to enjoy their rights, recourse mechanisms should be tailored to meet the needs of people experiencing discrimination and include appropriate safeguards. They should also be designed on the basis of a clear understanding of the nature of potential discrimination cases, such as which groups experience discrimination, in which sectors, for which occupations and for which employment processes, and the specific access barriers that are faced by these groups. This may require conducting specific surveys on legal needs in labour and employment, and strengthening the availability of the disaggregated data on cases, processes, their outcomes as well as the claimants.

Importantly, ADR settings in employment discrimination cases require adequate representation on both sides, adequate legal aid, and cultural and psychological adjustments to all forms of disadvantage. Legal assistance services should be sufficiently funded to ensure that such matters can be appropriately pursued where necessary. Adjusting ADR mechanisms to the profile of the employee and the harm

---

suffered can contribute to recognising the systemic nature of discrimination. At the same time, ADR mechanisms cannot be a mandatory alternative to litigation in cases of discrimination. When using the courts, however, there is a need to put in place active policies to remove the barriers to access, including the cost, complexity and length of procedures.

This Box is a contribution by the unit for Gender, Justice and Inclusiveness in the OECD Public Governance Directorate.

Affirmative action and hiring quotas

Affirmative action (AA) in hiring is broadly defined as policies addressing the under-representation of disadvantaged groups in the labour market through active measures that go beyond simple non-discrimination. In other words, AA instruments seek to increase the numbers of women and minorities in the workforce, most commonly by setting numerical targets including compulsory quotas, tie-break rules, and aspirational goals, which carry different levels of sanctions in case of non-compliance. Versions of affirmative action are found as "positive action" measures in European countries, where such policies are more recent and less extensively analysed than in the US context.

Under affirmative action legislation in the United States, federal contractors were required to implement affirmative action plans in a "good faith effort" in reaching certain targets to ensure representativeness in racial minority and female employment. Regular compliance reviews were an important factor for the effective implementation of affirmative action. Leonard (1990[11]) finds that among the firms subject to affirmative action policies within labour markets of the same industry and region, reviewed contractors fared better than the non-reviewed. Moreover, federal affirmative action requirements typically led to assignment of responsibility within the organisation to assure compliance, which has been another crucial factor for the successful implementation of affirmative action (Kalev, Dobbin and Kelly, 2006[12]). Finally, overall employment growth is a strong contextual factor influencing the success of affirmative action – evidence shows that such policies have been far more successful at growing establishments that have job openings to accommodate federal pressure (Leonard, 1990).

Overall, several studies show statistically significant shifts in the redistribution of jobs from white males to minorities and women following the introduction of federal affirmative action legislation (see Table 3.1). These beneficial effects for women and minority groups are persistent, as (Miller, 2017[13]) finds when examining the long-term effects of federal affirmative action regulation. The study, relying on turnover in public procurement relationships to compare contractors before and after falling under regulation to those firms that have never been contractors, indicates that the share of black employees continued to grow for more than a decade after a firm was deregulated. Research in the US context further suggests that following affirmative action legislation, which applied less forcefully to smaller firms with few employees, female and minority employment moved to larger firms. This transition to larger companies, which generally offer better pay, had a positive impact on women and minorities' wage growth (Carrington, McCue and Pierce, 2000[14]; Chay, 1998[15]).

Table 3.1. Studies on the impact of US federal affirmative action legislation on employment of female and racial minority workers

Author	Year of publication	Period analysed	Impact on labour market outcomes, by group
Ashenfelter et al	1976	1966 and 1970	Employment of Black male (+) relative to White male workers
Leonard	1985	1974-80	Growth in employment of White female (++) Black male (+) White male (-)
Holzer and Neumark	2000	Survey in 1992-94	Probability that White female (++), Black male (+), While male (-) are hired
Kalev et al.	2006	1971-2002	Managerial composition of Black males (+), Black females (/), White males (-), White females (++)
Kurtulus	2015	1973-2003	Within-firm share of Black workers (++), Native Americans (++) Hispanics (/), Asians (/), White female workers (-)
Miller	2017	1978-2004	Share of Black workers over time (+)

Note: (+) = impact is positive and statistically significant (++) = group with largest positive and significant impact; (-) = impact is negative and statistically significant; (/) = no impact.

In the context of positive action in Europe, countries are increasingly imposing concrete numerical goals on firms. Here, it is important to distinguish between *targets*, which are indicative, and *quotas*, which are compulsory (Heath, Liebig and Simon, 2013[10]). In the past 10 years, mandatory quotas for women in management boards and persons with disabilities have proliferated in the European context (see Table 3.2).

Table 3.2. Quotas for under-represented groups in the private sector

	Gender quota	Quota for people with disabilities
Austria	30% for boards of publicly listed companies and of companies with more than 1 000 employees	One disabled worker per 25 employees for all firms with at least 25 employees
Belgium	33% for management boards of public autonomous enterprises and for listed companies	/
Czech Republic	/	4% for all public and private sector firms with at least 25 employees
Germany	30% for supervisory boards of German enterprises (both private and public) quoted on the DAX stock exchange	5% for all public and private firms with at least 20 employees
France	40% for public limited companies, European companies and limited partnerships	6% for firms with at least 20 employees
Hungary	/	5% for all firms whose average number of employees exceeds 25 persons
Italy	33% for management boards of listed and publicly owned companies	7% for firms with more than 50 employees; at least 2 disabled workers for workplaces of 36 to 50 employees; at least 1 disabled worker if they operate new intake for firms of 15 to 35 employees
Japan	/	2.2% for all private firms with 45.5 or more workers
Portugal	33.3% for boards of directors and supervisory bodies of state-owned companies. For listed companies, the minimum is 20% in 2018 and rises to 33.3% in January 2020	/
Slovak Republic	/	3.2% for firms with at least 20 employees
Slovenia	/	3%, 6% or 9% depending on sector
Spain	/	2% for firms with at least 50 employees

Source: OECD "Diversity at Work" questionnaire.

Some countries, in contrast, set voluntary targets. The Swedish government, for example, suggests that 40% of management board members should be women; a similar target is set in the Netherlands. The Swedish government has also set the goal that at least 25% of newly recruited employees in the heavily male-dominated construction industry should be female by 2030. Furthermore, firms voluntarily self-regulate in many European OECD countries, stipulating non-binding targets in Corporate Governance Codes. However, only around 10% of respondents in our HR survey indicated that their firm had set targets for interviewing a certain minimum number of applicants from an under-represented group. The main groups for which these firms set interview target were women (76%), disabled people (39%), ethnic minorities (30%) and migrants (19%). Of Australian and Canadian firms with interview targets in place, 51% targeted indigenous populations.

Goals set in the context of affirmative action had a significant correlation with firms' improvement in employment of women and minorities in the United States (Leonard, 1985[16]). The impact in Europe is less researched, but voluntary targets adopted under Dutch affirmative action law Wet SAMEN had no significant effect on firms' end-of-year workforce composition (Groeneveld and Verbeek, 2012[17]). Unsurprisingly, non-binding targets are not being fulfilled with the same rigidity as are mandatory quotas. By way of example, the Norwegian gender quota requiring 40% females in company boards shows that under threat of dissolution of the board, which is foreseen in legislation in case of non-compliance, all companies ultimately complied. Female representation in Norwegian boards raised from less than 8% in 2002 to the required 40% after the deadline imposed by the law (Storvik and Teigen, 2010[18]). Similar results are found in the European comparison, where Germany, Belgium, France, and Italy have successfully increased the presence of female directors on boards through quota regulations (Horst and Wrohlich, 2018[19]).

The effectiveness of quotas in the European context is likely attributable to the strict sanctions imposed. A common sanction for firms that fail to comply with gender quotas in company boards is that any new appointment not in compliance with the respective law is automatically nullified. This so-called "empty chair rule" is applied in Austria, Germany and France. In Belgium, the law foresees the suspension of any financial or other benefits of all board members until the quota law has been complied with. In Italy, sanctions are applied progressively, starting from warnings, moving to fines and finally to forfeiture of the offices of all members of the board.

Firms that fail to comply with disability quotas generally incur financial penalties. Most commonly, countries have so-called "quota levy systems" in place – an equalisation mechanism that redistributes the funds raised from non-compliant firms to cover the costs of those firms that actually do employ disabled people. Some of the funds raised are also used for other purposes that further the labour market integration of disabled people. In some countries, firms that fail to hire the required number of disabled people can still be in compliance with quota. In France, firms can discharge their obligations to fulfil the disability quota by contributing into a fund for the promotion of employment of persons with disabilities. In Slovenia, firms can also partially outsource their activities to a company with more than 40% employees with disabilities.

The public discussion, however, is less centred around questions of effectiveness and focuses more on questions of fairness. This is particularly the case with regard to mandatory quotas, as the impossibility of ascertaining disadvantaged groups' counterfactual representation were there no discrimination inherently leads to suspicion that quotas excessively put minority groups at an advantage (Valfort, 2018[20]). This can trigger stigmatisation and backlash, as women and minorities may be perceived as receiving unfair preferential treatment or as being underqualified.

Furthermore, the overall positive effect of affirmative action must be qualified. While affirmative action leads to increases in employment for all groups, the extent of the benefit seems to differ, with some gaining significantly less than others. Evidence from the United States shows that the positive effect is strongest for White females, who account for more of the difference in employment rates following the introduction of affirmative action than do Black males, Black females or Hispanics (Leonard, 1985[16]; Holzer and Neumark, 2000[21]; Kalev, Dobbin and Kelly, 2006[12]). Why this is the case is more difficult to determine. White women, as the largest group of workers after White men, who are on average more highly educated and maybe more qualified than minorities, might be easier to recruit than other disadvantaged groups (Holzer and Neumark, 2000[21]).

The impact of affirmative action does not only differ between groups – a similar imbalance in advantage gained seems to hold for individuals within respective groups. For one, evaluations of the gender quotas in Norway and Italy have shown that the positive impact was confined to the direct effect on the women appointed for board management and that such policies had no impact on the advancement of the general female workforce of a firm (Maida and Weber, 2019[22]). Furthermore, critics argue that by targeting minority status rather than socio-economic factors, affirmative action benefits the most privileged middle- or upper-income brackets within minority groups at the expense of lower income ethnic minorities and lower-income White people (Kahlenberg (2012[23]), see Box 3.3).

Box 3.3. Socio-economic disadvantage as a ground for discrimination and positive action measures

Across the OECD, socio-economic background has a considerable impact on education and labour market outcomes. On average, it would take four to five generations for the offspring of a low-income family to reach the average income if levels of intergenerational mobility remain similar over time (OECD, 2018[24]).

Against this backdrop of low social mobility, socio-economic disadvantage remains an overlooked dimension of discrimination, despite evidence that (assumed) socio-economic status can harm candidates in the application process. Several CV testing studies in France and the United States have shown that fictitious candidates from disadvantaged neighbourhoods were less likely to be invited for interviews, also when names and free-time activities signalled that candidates were native-born and/or White (Bunel and Petit, 2016[25]; Bertrand and Mullainathan, 2004[26]). Findings for the United Kingdom show negative, but not significant results for 'postcode discrimination' associated with lower socio-economic status (Tunstall et al., 2014[27]; Nunn et al., 2010[28]). In 2019, 14 OECD countries explicitly acknowledge in their national non-discrimination legislation that socio-economic background can be a distinct ground for discrimination.

Yet, how to integrate socio-economic status into existing diversity policies is not straightforward. The main points of contention in this debate are well illustrated in the context of higher education in the United States, where there has been considerable criticism that college admission systems based solely on race would privilege the most economically advantaged minority students. Opponents of race-based affirmative action argue that, in a system based on socio-economic status (e.g. parental income, education or wealth), the most disadvantaged minorities would benefit, along with low-income White applicants (Sowell, 2004[29]).

One such alternative to race-based affirmative action, the "class-rank approach" replacing race-based approaches at US higher education institutions in some states, has found no support in the empirical literature. The impact of this system has been examined with evidence from public universities in Texas, to which pupils in the top ten percent of all schools in the state are guaranteed admission. This effectively enables students from disadvantaged schools with lower test scores to be admitted. Simulating the gains and losses associated with this policy regime, the authors find that race-blind admissions policies do not allow institutions to maintain the same level of racial diversity in higher education as with race-based systems, generally reducing the number of Black and Hispanic students (Harris and Tienda, 2010[30]).

This finding is in line with older studies in the US higher education context (Kane, 1998[31]; Cancian, 1998[32]; Carnevale and Rose, 2003[33]). While class-based approaches increase the number of qualified minority students, they significantly decrease their overall share of the qualified pool, since African Americans and Hispanics are disproportionately from low-SES families, but low-SES families are largely

---

white. Finding that income- and race-based policies have overlapping but not the same effects, Carnevale and Rose (2003[33]) advocate for a combination of both SES and minority status, i.e. SES as a supplement, but not a replacement of race-based admissions. Hence, SES-based policies are not an effective substitute for reaching racial and ethnic enrolment goals, unless low-income minorities can be chosen disproportionately from the qualified pool of low-SES students.

Financial incentives and public procurement

Given that the business case at the firm level is not always clear-cut, financial incentives to hire disadvantaged groups can be a means to strengthen the business case for employers under certain conditions. Similarly, public procurement regulations that promote supplier diversity can be an important policy tool, seeing that OECD countries spent around 12% of GDP on goods and services through public procurement in 2016 (OECD, 2017[34]).

Using public procurement as a strategic tool to strengthen diversity and equal treatment is a fairly widespread policy approach in OECD countries (see Figure 3.3), mostly with regard to incentivising the hiring of women and employees with disabilities. Some governments give preference to firms in cases of tie-break between applications for public funds, e.g. in Latvia, others grant extra points in point-based contract award systems, as is the case in Japan and Mexico. In addition, many EU OECD countries, where public procurement is regulated by both domestic and EU law, follow the clauses for "social considerations" stipulated in the EU public procurement Directive of 2014 (2014/24/EU). These allow Member States the option to consider participation of vulnerable and disadvantaged people in the award of contracts as well as the possibility to reserve procurement procedures to social enterprises working for the inclusion of disadvantaged people.

Figure 3.3. Diversity criteria considered in public procurement

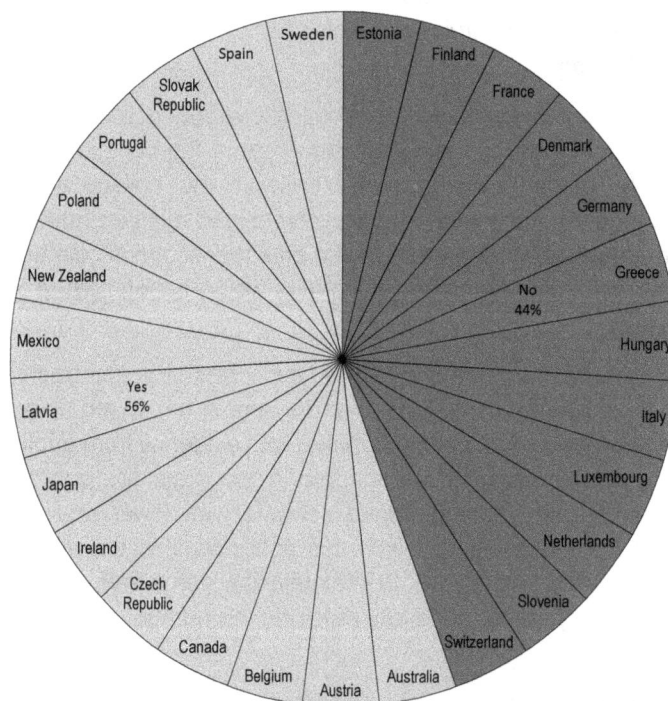

Note: This includes countries that allow for social considerations in public procurement rather than making this a mandatory component of public tenders.
Source: OECD "Diversity at Work" questionnaire.

Some countries have stronger and more concrete obligations in this regard. Australia has set a target in procurement – the *Commonwealth Indigenous Procurement Policy* requires that by 2020, 3% of Federal Government contracts each year be sourced from indigenous suppliers. In Canada, all contractors must sign an *Agreement to Implement Employment Equity* within 30 days of contract award. As per the agreement, firms are required to make reasonable efforts to ensure progress is made towards having full representation of women, disabled people, and members of visible minorities and indigenous people within their workforce. Progress is reviewed through regular compliance assessments by the Labour Program. Failure to adhere to the requirements can result in the loss of the current contract and/or in the contractor losing the right to bid on future contracts.

Governments using public procurement to support diversity objectives should, however, also consider the risk of disrupting the efficiency of public procurement. The expenses and trade-offs, if they exist, must be evaluated, assessing whether procurement is the most cost-effective way to achieve specific diversity objectives (OECD, 2017[35]; 2013[36]).

Subsidising wages in the employment of under-represented groups is another means by which OECD governments seek to strengthen the business case for diversity with regard to workers with disabilities, as well as migrant and older workers. There are two types of wage subsidies: Hiring subsidies are granted temporarily, whereas employment subsidies are provided over an extended period of time or indefinitely. While the latter assumes a permanent productivity gap, temporary subsidy schemes that phase-out after time follow the rationale that on-the-job training of certain groups takes more time, but that the productivity gap can eventually be closed. Temporary subsidies can also reduce the initial insecurity with regard to the actual productivity, lowering the costs that a "trial phase" imposes on employers. Across OECD countries, subsidies vary in type (wages and/or social security contributions) and the amount of labour cost compensated.

Wage subsidies are a long-standing component of active labour market policies to strengthen the employment of low-wage workers, long-term unemployed and young job seekers in OECD countries. A rich literature on the impact of such subsidies on the employment of disadvantaged groups has developed, highlighting the difficulties of getting incentives 'right'. Issues with wage subsidies include risks of stigmatisation, substitution and displacement effects as well as dead-weight losses, i.e. providing subsidies to firms that would have hired workers without these financial incentives.

The effectiveness of subsidies for older workers has been investigated through studies of such schemes in Germany, Finland and Belgium. The evidence suggest that for these groups, the deadweight effect is high, meaning that employers' decisions are unchanged in comparison to a hypothetical situation in which the subsidy is not paid. It also appears that generally, subsidised work simply displaces unsubsidised work, with little net gain in terms of employment (Boockmann, 2015[37]).

Although rarely explicitly targeting migrants, wage subsidies have proven effective for this group. A meta-analysis by Butschek and Walter (2014[38]) on interventions in Nordic countries, Germany, the Netherlands and Switzerland finds that effect estimates for wage subsidy programmes are mostly positive, suggesting that such subsidies are indeed a promising measure to increase employment rates of immigrants. Migrants, however, tend to be underrepresented among beneficiaries of such schemes, possibly because they themselves or employers do not know about their eligibility (OECD, 2014[39]).

Other studies on subsidies for workers with disabilities show that some of the general risks around active labour market policy, e.g. regarding deadweight or substitution effects, is less relevant for this group, because of the permanent productivity loss of some groups of people with disabilities (OECD, 2003[40]). Especially for this group, schemes must consider that persons with disabilities are a very heterogeneous group. People have different types of disabilities and these can be more or less severe and can be acquired at birth or later in life. Persons with disabilities also vary in other demographic characteristics to which the subsidies should be well-targeted. For example, age seems to be an important factor determining if subsidies are successful or counterproductive and stigmatising (Deuchert and Kauer, 2017[41]). The level of subsidy should be dependent on the capacity of the worker as well as flexible, as work capacity of persons with disabilities may also change over time. On the other hand, subsidies might be needed for a long period and even a permanent subsidy might be justified in some cases (OECD, 2010[42]).

OECD countries also offer financial compensation and rewards to firms for taking action beyond hiring disadvantaged groups. One such instrument are accommodation subsidies. Slovakia, for example, provides cash allowances for firms that wish to establish sheltered workplaces, hire a personal assistant for a disabled employee, or facilitate their transport. Another type of incentives seeks to encourage disadvantaged groups' career development. Japan, for instance, offers subsidy schemes providing a financial reward to employers that achieve a self-imposed numerical target for the advancement of female employees set in action plans. A majority of countries also provides non-financial incentives (see Box 3.4).

Box 3.4. Rewarding 'diversity champions' through awards and labels

Providing awards and labels to firms that have implemented comprehensive diversity strategies is fairly widespread across OECD countries. The rationale behind this is often to create awareness of good practices and reward business for inclusive policies as 'leading by example.' For companies themselves, the motivation of participating in an award or labelling process may also be related to brand management, raising their visibility and attracting more talent.

A number of countries have annual awards that are given to companies on behalf of the government or Ministries. Most of these awards, e.g. in Australia, Spain, Portugal and Slovakia, concern policies that seek to promote gender equality based on selection criteria such as work-life balance, parental leave policies and flexible work arrangements. In addition, some awards take into account other grounds, e.g. Slovenia granting senior-friendly company awards and Mexico providing diversity awards based on multiple grounds, including, amongst others, ethnic and indigenous minorities and LGBT people. The UK Civil Service rewards individual public servants who have acted as 'diversity champions' within the civil services, including on LGBT inclusion, race equality, gender, disability and socio-economic status.

In addition to governments, numerous NGO initiatives, HR associations and social partners seek to promote and reward inclusive businesses. For instance, so-called Diversity Charters – with currently 21 national organisations in the EU and an EU platform serving as umbrella organisation – encourage firms to sign their charter, pledging to advance diversity and inclusion through concrete workplace policies. Overall, more than 10 000 firms are signatories to these charters, representing almost 15 million employees in the EU.

Furthermore, a number of countries have developed certification procedures and diversity labels that are granted usually for two to three years before the certification is re-assessed. France, for example, introduced the so-called Diversity Label in 2008, together with social partners and the national HR association (ANDRH). Firms applying for this label undergo a 'diversity audit' conducted by the French Standardisation Association (AFNOR). As of 2018, around 300 companies had received this label, representing around 1.3 million workers. AFNOR also provides a label specifically for promoting gender equality. A similar label is provided by the Brussels-Capital region, Estonia and Latvia. In Latvia, for example, companies can receive a "family-friendly company status" if they have implemented measures around work-life balance, flexible working hours and health protection in the workplace, while Slovenia provides a label for disability inclusion at the workplace.

Outreach to under-represented groups

The importance of networks in finding employment is well established; social and professional networks may not only help for being referred and making personal connections, but also for obtaining information on job openings in the first place. Groups traditionally disadvantaged in the labour market may not have these connections. For example, people with a migrant background and ethnic minorities tend to have fewer contacts with people in higher social positions (Li, Savage and Warde (2008[43]) for the United Kingdom); get fewer job leads (McDonald, Lin and Ao (2009[44]) for the United States); and receive less help from their social network when applying for apprenticeships (Beicht and Granato (2010[45]) for Germany). Thus, an important component of diversity policies is to mitigate this initial disadvantage and increase the pool of qualified candidates through proactive outreach measures. In a number of OECD countries, such campaigns have been developed, often on a city or regional level, specifically targeting candidates with a migration background (see Box 3.5).

In addition, outreach to underrepresented groups can address barriers that are not only related to a lack of networks, but also to gender stereotypes about what are perceived as typically male and female jobs, leading to fewer candidates in STEM jobs for women and education and care for men. For instance, 5.5% of male workers in OECD countries are ICT specialists, compared to only 1.4% of female workers. At the same time, women remain strongly over-represented in the education and care sector; among primary school teachers, more than four in five are women (OECD, 2017[46]).

Difficulties in increasing the applicant pool also became apparent in the findings of the HR survey. When asked about the main difficulties faced while implementing diversity measures, the most common obstacle named was that too few qualified candidates from disadvantaged groups applied (47%).

The majority of HR representatives believe that outreach campaigns would help their company increase diversity (see Figure 3.4). Nevertheless, only 20% of all firms surveyed indicated that they have implemented outreach or recruitment campaigns targeting under-represented groups. Partly, this reflect that outreach campaigns are costly to implement and may not be feasible for smaller companies; of the firms with diversity measures, only 20% of firms with less than 250 employees had outreach measures in place, compared to 40% among firms with over 250 employees.

Figure 3.4. A majority of HR representatives think that outreach campaigns would help their company recruit disadvantaged groups

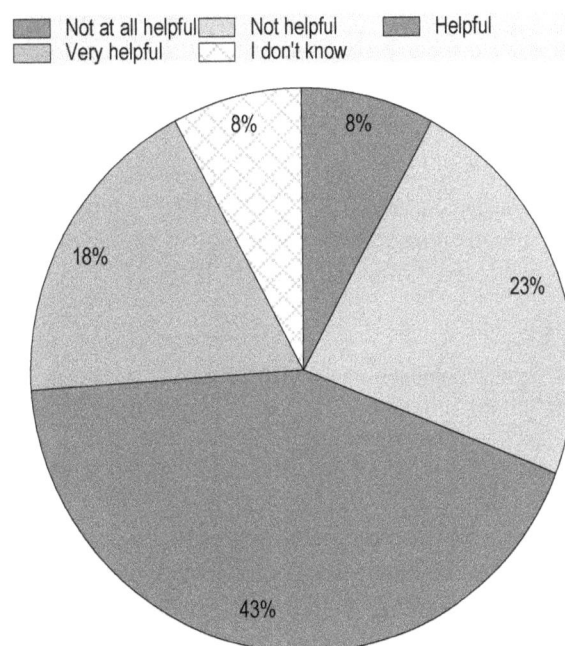

Source: OECD-Dauphine HR Survey.

Many public administrations in OECD countries have implemented outreach campaigns and traineeship programmes targeting specific groups with the aim of building a workforce that is more representative of the public they serve.

Most outreach campaigns for the public sector tend to be concentrated in education, targeting pupils and recent or soon-to-be university graduates. In Australia, specific programmes seek to encourage Aboriginal and/or Torres Strait university graduates, as well as graduates with a disability into the Australian Public Service (APS). Similarly, the Swiss public administration cooperates with specific universities to recruit more women. In some countries, such programmes begin as early as during secondary education. In Estonia, campaigns in Russian language schools seek to encourage pupils of Russian nationality to apply for the public service. The French public service offers 15 000 internships in the public administration to students around age 15 who attend schools with high shares of disadvantaged students (schools in the *réseau d'éducation prioritaire renforcé).*

Recruiters for the public administration use a wide range of channels to reach diverse groups. The Irish Public Appointments Service, for example, has engaged in a number of activities to communicate job opportunities to underrepresented groups over social media including Facebook, Twitter and LinkedIn, targeting a range of nationalities and Travellers, LGBT people, disabled people and Irish language groups. In the Netherlands, public authorities work with professional migrant or diversity networks and student associations to encourage highly educated young people with a non-Western migration background to apply for jobs in the public administration. Integrating such local stakeholders into efforts to approach hard-to-reach groups is crucial, especially with regard to youth from migrant families (OECD, forthcoming[47]).

Box 3.5. Reaching out to young people with a migrant background

In a number of OECD countries, outreach campaigns have targeted young people with a migrant background to apply for apprenticeships and jobs.

The state of Hamburg, for example, has launched the campaign "We are Hamburg" (*Wir sind Hamburg)* encouraging young people with a migration background to apply for internships in the public administration. Similarly, the state of Berlin has launched the campaign "Berlin needs you" (*Berlin braucht dich*). The initiative works through a network of 30 schools and 60 companies, providing career guidance, organising side visits and running trainings and information sessions.

In addition, a number of initiatives have focused specifically on diversifying the police force through outreach campaigns, including for example in the city of Vienna, Chicago and London. In addition, 14 out of the 16 German regional states have outreach activities in place for recruiting more people with a migrant background for the police force (Ghelli and Pross, 2019[48]).

Anonymous job applications

Anonymous or "blind" job applications are aimed at reducing bias in the application process by removing information that could activate recruiters' stereotypes, such as 'foreign-sounding' names, gender, age or address. Used only by 6% of firms that have diversity measures in place, anonymous applications were not a common instrument in the HR survey sample. Those firms that did hide characteristics in the hiring process, most often removed an applicant's age, followed by their name and address (see Figure 3.5). Another commonly masked characteristic was civil or marital status. Almost 19% of those firms implementing diversity measures stated that their application process does not require a photograph of the candidate, despite this being common practice within the industry or country concerned.

Figure 3.5. CV information hidden to recruiters in anonymous application procedures

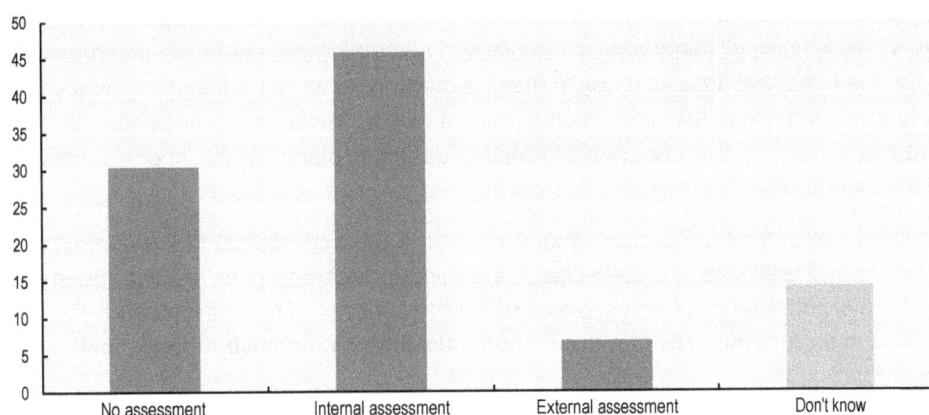

Note: Number of firms; n=79 (companies with anonymous CV procedures in place).
Source: OECD-Dauphine HR Survey.

In several European countries including Sweden, France, the Netherlands and Germany, the effects of anonymous job applications have been tested in field experiments. The French government has conducted an experiment with jobseekers registered with the public employment service in 2010 and 2011 involving around 1 000 firms for a period of ten months. The result was that women benefited from higher call-back rates. Surprisingly, the second finding was that immigrants and residents of deprived neighbourhoods suffered from anonymous job applications, as their call-back rates were lower with anonymous job applications than with standard applications (Behaghel, Crépon and Le Barbanchon, 2011[49]). The gap in interview rate between minority and majority candidates widened by around 10 percentage points when CVs were anonymised. The effect seemed to persist beyond the application screening stage, as the hiring gap also widened by four points (only significant at the 10% level).

A second experiment was conducted by the Swedish city of Gothenburg between 2004 and 2006, which introduced a pilot project to test the impact of anonymous CVs on hiring outcomes. Based on a difference-in-differences analysis of around 3 500 applications made to around 100 job openings in the local administration, Åslund and Skans (2012[50]) find that anonymous job applications increased the chances of an interview invitation for both women and applicants of non-Western origin when compared to standard applications, by the same order of magnitude for both groups. These increased chances for candidates in the first stage translated into a higher job offer rate for women, but not for migrants, suggesting that barriers at the interview stage are more difficult to remove for the latter group. The authors speculate that the high importance placed on gender equality in the Swedish context may have influenced the findings.

Studies on further trials, including small-scale pilots within single organisations, did not yield statistically significant effects. Nevertheless, they give indications of how diverse the effects of anonymous applications can be depending on the groups concerned (see for example Krause, Rinne and Zimmermann (2011[51])). A common explanation for the contradicting findings in the literature is the crucial importance of the initial situation in the respective industry or organisation. While effective in the face of bias and discriminatory practices, anonymity prevents employers committed to diversity from *favouring* minority applicants when credentials are equal. In situations where such affirmative action practices are in place, the introduction of anonymous job applications may cause interview invitation probabilities of minority groups to decrease. Anonymous applications might be helpful with regard to biases, but unproductive when it comes to structural disadvantages, since they remove characteristics that could serve to explain subpar labour market outcomes from the process.

Current evidence does therefore not support the introduction of anonymous job applications in every context. Anonymous hiring might be sensible in a specific sector or for a certain company where there is sizeable discrimination, but be futile where there is no discrimination, and even counterproductive where practices of favouring women or minorities are in place. This finding relates to the limitation of the studies discussed above: the firms and organisations in these experiments were participating on a voluntary basis. There has likely been firm selection into such programmes by those already concerned with diversity issues, who are more likely to already have affirmative action in place, which might explain some of the negative results.

Removing bias from the recruitment process has also been a topic of interest in the context of data-driven HR practices. HR analytics aim to use statistical (data mining) techniques to predict uncertain outcomes, i.e. the performance of potential employees, and monitor the success of recruitment and retention. Through predictive analytics in recruitment, HR can draw upon data-driven predictive models, instead of relying on gut feeling and soft science.

Such new technologies are already impacting the labour market, with the potential to counteract discrimination and unconscious bias in hiring. Two recent studies provide experimental evidence on the impact of algorithms on the probability that atypical job candidates are hired. In both cases the software favoured "non-traditional" candidates, in contrast to human screeners. The algorithm exhibited significantly less bias against candidates that were underrepresented at the firm, such as those without personal referrals or degrees from prestigious universities (Cowgill, 2018[52]; Hoffman, Kahn and Li, 2018[53]). Another recent study finds that compared to those candidates chosen by humans, board directors selected by algorithms were less likely to be male and had smaller networks (Erel et al., 2018[54]).

However, it must be kept in mind that algorithms are not necessarily free of bias, as they are written and maintained by people, and machine learning algorithms adjust what they do based on people's behaviour. Although not designed with the intent of discriminating against certain groups, algorithms are likely to incorporate historical prejudices if the training data reflect existing social biases against a minority (Goodman, 2016[55]). Nevertheless, the more relevant question for practitioners and policy makers concerned with diversity and anti-discrimination is to ask how algorithms compare with the status quo – and the evidence suggests that HR analytics has the potential to make some decisions exhibiting less bias than humans do.

Diversity training

Creating an inclusive workplace is a crucial step in making the most of diversity. All efforts put into hiring diverse candidates are fruitless if these workers cannot flourish or end up leaving the organisation for feeling excluded at the workplace. To this end, diversity training encompasses a wide array of programmes intended to train managers' and employees' attitudes, reduce stereotypes and enhance their skills in dealing with diversity. Such trainings were found to be in widespread use in the HR survey – 44% of firms with measures in place have implemented trainings for all employees, and 20% have specific training for HR personnel. The overwhelming majority of HR representatives surveyed stated that a wider availability of training could help their company increase diversity (see Figure 3.6). In the academic literature, diversity training has generally been found to have no impact on the representation of disadvantaged groups (Kalev, Dobbin and Kelly, 2006[12]), while the impact on attitudes towards diversity varies from beneficial in some contexts to no or a relatively modest negative effect in others (Kulik and Roberson, 2008[56]).

Kulik et al. (2007[57]) find that voluntary diversity training likely attracts those employees who need training the least. Because employees who are sceptical towards diversity are usually not able to gauge their own competence in dealing with diversity, they assess their need to develop those skills inadequately. This means that voluntary training often misses those employees with lowest skill competencies. While pre-training competence of (potential) participants matters, demographics have non-significant effects on interest in training and participation. This means that women, ethnic minorities and older employees do not seem more open towards voluntary training on diversity issues than are other employees.

Implementing mandatory diversity training may avoid 'preaching to the choir', yet it is unclear whether they are more effective, as external control and perceived societal pressure were found to have a negative effect on training outcomes (Legault, Gutsell and Inzlicht, 2011[58]).

Figure 3.6. An overwhelming majority of HR representatives think that wider availability of diversity trainings would be helpful to increase diversity in their company

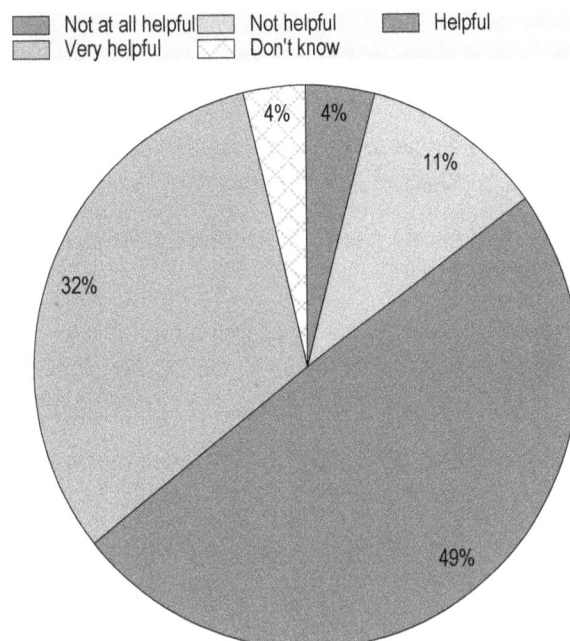

Source: OECD-Dauphine HR Survey.

Several studies examine how training should be designed to affect participants' attitude and skill outcomes positively, showing that diversity training needs to stimulate intrinsic motivation rather than framing it around social norms. Legault et al. provided participants with instructions that either encouraged autonomous motivation to regulate prejudice by emphasising the value of non-prejudice, or imposed control of prejudice, framing it as a societal requirement to comply with norms. The results show that external control to reduce prejudice produces more bias than not intervening at all. (Kulik, Perry and Bourhis, 2000[59]) find that under certain circumstances, instructing participants to *suppress* age-related stereotypes activated them in the first place, thus creating unintended negative consequences for the evaluation of older applicants. Similarly, instructing participants to simply discard their bias as "wrong" without adequately addressing and deconstructing it seems to leave participants more confused and more biased towards diverse groups (Dobbin and Kalev, 2018[60]).

The duration of training is another important factor. To be effective in the long-run, training must be sustained over an extended period, as effects are found to dissipate within short time periods, often within days (Paluck and Green, 2009[61]). Devine et al. (2012[62]) develop a multi-faceted prejudice habit-breaking intervention to produce long-term reductions in implicit race bias. The 12-week longitudinal study comparing a group of people who completed the intervention to a control group who did not showed that sustained training leads to increased concern about discrimination and personal awareness of bias. For most participants, the effect on implicit bias control lasted throughout the eight week interval observed in the aftermath of the intervention. Such repeated, longer-term trainings, however, are a costly undertaking that firms are unlikely to implement.

In view of the volatile nature of training effects, diversity training can only be one element of a wider set of policies. As a one-time, standalone measure, it is unlikely to have any substantial impact on attitudes. Diversity training might get the conversation on existing bias started, but must be combined with other, more structural measures (Dobbin and Kalev, 2018[60]) suggest that firms must actively engage managers in reducing bias within their workforce, including them as "diversity champions" in an overall positive message. The close interaction with women and minorities in mentoring and college recruitment schemes, for example, seem to be more effective in reducing managers' bias than diversity training.

References

Acemoglu, D. and J. Angrist (2001), "Consequences of Employment Protection? The Case of the Americans with Disabilities Act", *Journal of Political Economy*, Vol. 109/5. [7]

Åslund, O. and O. Skans (2012), "Do Anonymous Job Application Procedures Level the Playing Field?", *ILR Review*, Vol. 65/1, pp. 82-107. [50]

Balestra, C. and L. Fleischer (2018), "Diversity statistics in the OECD: How do OECD countries collect data on ethnic, racial and indigenous identity?", *OECD Statistics Working Papers*, No. 2018/09, OECD Publishing, Paris, https://dx.doi.org/10.1787/89bae654-en. [3]

Behaghel, L., B. Crépon and T. Le Barbanchon (2011), *Evaluation de l'impact du CV anonyme*, Paris School of Economics. [49]

Beicht, U. and M. Granato (2010), *Ausbildungsplatzsuche: Geringere Chancen für junge Frauen und Männer mit Migrationshintergrund – BIBB-Analyse zum Einfluss der sozialen Herkunft beim Übergang in die Ausbildung unter Berücksichtigung von Geschlecht und Migrationsstatus*, Bundesinstitut für Berufsbildung, BIBB Report: Forschungs- und Arbeitsergebnisse aus dem Bundesinstitut für Berufsbildung, No. 15. [45]

Bertrand, M. and S. Mullainathan (2004), "Are Emily and Greg More Employable Than Lakisha and Jamal? A Field Experiment on Labor Market Discrimination", *American Economic Review*, Vol. 94/4, pp. 991-1013. [26]

Boockmann, B. (2015), "The effects of wage subsidies for older workers", No. 189, IZA World of Labor. [37]

Bunel, M. and P. Petit (2016), "Discrimination based on place of residence and access to employment", *Urban Studies Journal Limited*, Vol. 53/2, pp. 267-286. [25]

Butschek, S. and T. Walter (2014), "What active labour market programmes work for immigrants in Europe? A meta-analysis of the evaluation literature", *IZA Journal of Migration*, Vol. 48/3. [38]

Cancian, M. (1998), "Race-based versus class-based affirmative action in college admissions", *Journal of Policy Analysis and Management*, Vol. 17/1, pp. 94-105. [32]

Carnevale, A. and S. Rose (2003), "Socioeconomic Status, Race/Ethnicity, and Selective College Admissions", Century Foundation. [33]

Carrington, W., K. McCue and B. Pierce (2000), "Using Establishment Size to Measure the Impact of Title VII and Affirmative Action", *The Journal of Human Resources*, Vol. 35/3, pp. 503-525.　[14]

Chay, K. (1998), "The Impact of Federal Civil Rights Policy on Black Economic Progress: Evidence from the Equal Employment Opportunity Act of 1972", *ILR Review*, Vol. 51/4, pp. 608-632.　[15]

Cialdini, R. and N. Goldstein (2004), "Social Influence: Compliance and Conformity", *Annual Review of Psychology*, Vol. 55/1, pp. 591-621.　[9]

Cowgill, B. (2018), "Bias and Productivity in Humans and Algorithms: Theory and Evidence from Résumé Screening", Columbia University Working Paper.　[52]

Crenshaw, K. (1989), "Demarginalizing the Intersection of Race and Sex: A Black Feminist Critique of Antidiscrimination Doctrine, Feminist Theory and Antiracist Politics", *Univesity of Chicago Legal Forum*, Vol. 1, Article 8.　[1]

Deuchert, E. and L. Kauer (2017), "Hiring subsidies for people with a disability: Evidence from a small-scale social field experiment", *International Labour Review*, Vol. 156/2, pp. 269-285.　[41]

Devine, P. et al. (2012), "Long-term reduction in implicit race bias: A prejudice habit-breaking intervention.", *Journal of Experimental Social Psychology*, Vol. 48/6, pp. 1267-1278.　[62]

Dobbin, F. and A. Kalev (2018), "Why Doesn't Diversity Training Work? The Challenge for Industry and Academia", *Anthropology Now*, Vol. 10/2, pp. 48-55.　[60]

Donohue, J. (2005), "The Law and Economics of Antidiscrimination Law", *Yale Law & Economics Research Paper*, No. 318.　[5]

Erel, I. et al. (2018), "Selecting Directors Using Machine Learning", *NBER Working Paper*, No. w24435.　[54]

Ghelli, F. and J. Pross (2019), "Interkulturelle Öffnung. Die Polizei wird vielfältiger", *Mediendienst Integration*, https://mediendienst-integration.de/artikel/die-polizei-wird-vielfaeltiger.html.　[48]

Goodman, B. (2016), *Economic Models of (Algorithmic) Discrimination*.　[55]

Groeneveld, S. and S. Verbeek (2012), "Diversity Policies in Public and Private Sector Organizations: An Empirical Comparison of Incidence and Effectiveness", *Review of Public Personnel Administration*, Vol. 32/4, pp. 353-381.　[17]

Harris, A. and M. Tienda (2010), "Minority Higher Education Pipeline: Consequences of Changes in College Admissions Policy in Texas", *The ANNALS of the American Academy of Political and Social Science*, Vol. 627/1, pp. 60-81.　[30]

Heath, Liebig and Simon (2013), *Discrimination against immigrants – measurement, incidence and policy instruments*, OECD Publishing, Paris, https://dx.doi.org/10.1787/migr_outlook-2013-en.　[10]

Hoffman, M., L. Kahn and D. Li (2018), "Discretion in Hiring", *The Quarterly Journal of Economics*, Vol. 133/2, pp. 765-800.　[53]

Holzer, H. and D. Neumark (2000), "What does affirmative action do?", *Industrial and Labor Relations Review*, Vol. 53/2, pp. 240-271.　[21]

Horst, E. and K. Wrohlich (2018), "Spitzengremien großer Unternehmen: Geschlechterquote für Aufsichtsräte greift, in Vorständen herrscht beinahe Stillstand", *Deutsches Institut für Wirtschaftsforschung: Managerinnen-Barometer: Unternehmen*. [19]

Kahlenberg, R. (2012), *A Better Affirmative Action: State Universities that Created Alternatives to Racial Preferences*, Century Foundation. [23]

Kalev, A., F. Dobbin and E. Kelly (2006), "Best Practices or Best Guesses? Assessing the Efficacy of Corporate Affirmative Action and Diversity Policies", *American Sociological Review*, Vol. 71, pp. 589-617. [12]

Kane, T. (1998), "Racial and Ethnic Preferences in College Admissions", *Ohio State Law Journal*, Vol. 59/3, pp. 971-996. [31]

Krause, A., U. Rinne and K. Zimmermann (2011), "Anonymous Job Applications of Fresh Ph.D. Economists", No. 6100, IZA Discussion Paper. [51]

Kulik, C. et al. (2007), "The rich get richer: predicting participation in voluntary diversity training", *Journal of Organizational Behavior*, Vol. 28/6, pp. 753-769. [57]

Kulik, C., E. Perry and A. Bourhis (2000), "Ironic Evaluation Processes: Effects of Thought Suppression on Evaluations of Older Job", *Journal of Organizational Behavior*, Vol. 21/6, pp. 689-711. [59]

Kulik, C. and L. Roberson (2008), "Common Goals and Golden Opportunities: Evaluations of Diversity Education in Academic and Organizational Settings", *Academy of Management Learning & Education*, Vol. 7/3, pp. 309-331. [56]

Legault, L., J. Gutsell and M. Inzlicht (2011), "Ironic Effects of Antiprejudice Messages: How Motivational Interventions Can Reduce (But Also Increase) Prejudice", *Psychological Science*, Vol. 22/12, pp. 1472-1477. [58]

Leonard, J. (1990), "The Impact of Affirmative Action Regulation and Equal Employment Law on Black", *The Journal of Economic Perspectives*, Vol. 4/4, pp. 47-63. [11]

Leonard, J. (1985), "What Promises Are Worth: The Impact of Affirmative Action Goals", *Source: The Journal of Human Resources*, Vol. 20/1, pp. 3-20. [16]

Li, Y., M. Savage and A. Warde (2008), "Social mobility and social capital in contemporary Britain", *British Journal of Sociology*, Vol. 59/3, pp. 391-411. [43]

Maida, A. and A. Weber (2019), "Female Leadership and Gender Gap within Firms: Evidence from an Italian Board Reform", *Discussion Paper Series*, IZA Institute of Labor Economics. [22]

Makkonen, T. (2016), *European handbook on equality data 2016 revision*, Publications Office of the European Union, Luxembourg. [4]

McDonald, S., N. Lin and D. Ao (2009), "Networks of opportunity: Gender, race, and job leads", *Social Problems*, Vol. 56/3, pp. 385-402. [44]

Miller, C. (2017), "The Persistent Effect of Temporary Affirmative Action", *American Economic Journal: Applied Economics*, Vol. 9/3, pp. 152-190. [13]

Nunn, A. et al. (2010), *Postcode selection? Employers' use of area-and address-based information shortcuts in recruitment decisions*, Department for Work and Pensions. [28]

OECD (2018), *A Broken Social Elevator? How to Promote Social Mobility*, OECD Publishing, Paris, http://dx.doi.org/10.1787/9789264301085-en. [24]

OECD (2017), *Government at a Glance 2017*, OECD Publishing, Paris, https://dx.doi.org/10.1787/gov_glance-2017-en. [34]

OECD (2017), "OECD Framework to Promote the Strategic Use of Public Procurement for Innovation", in *Public Procurement for Innovation: Good Practices and Strategies*, OECD Publishing, Paris, https://dx.doi.org/10.1787/9789264265820-6-en. [35]

OECD (2017), *The Pursuit of Gender Equality. An Uphill Battle*, http://dx.doi.org/10.1787/9789264281318-en (accessed on 5 October 2017). [46]

OECD (2014), *International Migration Outlook 2014*, OECD Publishing, Paris, https://dx.doi.org/10.1787/migr_outlook-2014-en. [39]

OECD (2013), "A strategic role for public procurement", in *Implementing the OECD Principles for Integrity in Public Procurement: Progress since 2008*, OECD Publishing, Paris, https://dx.doi.org/10.1787/9789264201385-7-en. [36]

OECD (2010), *Sickness, Disability and Work: Breaking the Barriers: A Synthesis of Findings across OECD Countries*, OECD Publishing, Paris, https://dx.doi.org/10.1787/9789264088856-en. [42]

OECD (2008), *OECD Employment Outlook 2008*, OECD Publishing, Paris, https://dx.doi.org/10.1787/empl_outlook-2008-en. [6]

OECD (2003), *Transforming Disability into Ability: Policies to Promote Work and Income Security for Disabled People*, OECD Publishing, Paris, https://dx.doi.org/10.1787/9789264158245-en. [40]

OECD (forthcoming), *Making Integration Work: Young people with a migrant background*, OECD Publishing, Paris. [47]

Paluck, E. and D. Green (2009), "Prejudice Reduction: What Works? A Review and Assessment of Research and Practice", *Annual Review of Psychology*, Vol. 60/1, pp. 339-367. [61]

Sowell, T. (2004), *Affirmative action around the world: An empirical study*, Yale University Press. [29]

Storvik, A. and M. Teigen (2010), *Women on board - the Norwegian experience*, Friedrich Ebert Stiftung. [18]

Tankard, M. and E. Paluck (2017), "The Effect of a Supreme Court Decision Regarding Gay Marriage on Social Norms and Personal Attitudes", *Psychological Science*, Vol. 28/9, pp. 1334-1344. [8]

Tunstall, R. et al. (2014), "Does poor neighbourhood reputation create a neighbourhood effect on employment? The results of a field experiment in the UK", *Urban Studies*, Vol. 51/4, pp. 763-780. [27]

Valfort, M. (2018), "Do anti-discrimination policies work?", No. 450, IZA World of Labor. [20]

Valfort, M. (2015), "Religious discrimination in access to employment: a reality", No. October 2015, Institut Montaigne. [2]

4 Challenges in promoting effective diversity policies

This chapter discusses challenges in promoting effective diversity policies. There is a limited evidence base on what works on the ground, for which groups and under what kind of circumstances. Furthermore, the implementation of policies may raise problems; SMEs may face particular difficulties in implementing diversity policies and appear to be less likely to do so. Given that diversity policies are often subject to heated debate, policy makers and employers may also have to anticipate and manage negative reactions, to ensure that policies are not having unintended detrimental effects. Lastly, the chapter discusses the common criticism that diversity policies are often adopted as a means for image management and branding, with little regard for their actual impact. Ensuring that diversity policies are actually impactful and go beyond window-dressing is a critical concern going forward.

Gathering data on diversity and measuring the impact of policies

Currently, the evidence base on 'what works' is still relatively small and the success of programmes usually differ across different national contexts and groups targeted. Gathering data on diversity in the workplace is the first step in assessing whether diversity policies are effective. However, in most countries, the collection of data on diversity is limited (see Table 4.1). Most countries that have introduced requirements for firms to monitor composition and pay of their workforce have done this for data collection on gender, age and, to some extent, disability.

Table 4.1. Requirements to provide diversity data on employees in the private sector

OECD country	Data on	For some companies	For certain positions	By seniority level
Australia	Gender	Non-public sector employers with 100 or more employees	-	No
Austria	Gender	Companies with 150 or more employees	-	Indirectly
Belgium	No obligation			
Canada	Gender, Disability, Visible minorities and Indigenous Peoples	Federally regulated private-sector employers subject to the Legislated Employment Equity Program (LEEP)	-	Yes
Czech Republic	Gender, Nationality, Age, Disability	-	-	No
Denmark	Gender	Companies with a balance sum on 156 mil. DKK; a revenue on 313 mil. DKK; an average of 250 full-time employees	Highest management body	No
Estonia	Gender, Age	Enterprises owned by the government and local authorities with a minimum of 50 employees	-	Yes
Finland	Gender, Age	Firms whose number of personnel working for an employer on a regular basis is at least 30		Yes
France	Gender, Age, Disability, Geographic zone	companies whose securities are admitted to trading on a regulated market and / or companies exceeding certain thresholds of turnover, balance sheet total and / number of employees	-	No
Germany	Gender, Nationality, Age	-	-	No
Greece	**No obligation**			
Hungary	Disability	Firms employing people with disability		No
Ireland	**No obligation**			
Italy	Gender, Nationality, Age, Disability	-	-	Yes
Japan	Nationality, Age, Disability	-	-	No
Latvia	**No obligation**			
Lithuania	**No obligation**			
Luxembourg	**No obligation**			
Mexico	**No obligation**			
Netherlands	**No obligation**			
New Zealand	**No obligation**			
Poland	Gender, Nationality, Age, Disability	All firms with 25 or more employees, all employers of the sheltered labour market and those employers who apply for wage subsidies	-	Indirectly
Portugal	Gender	State-owned companies and listed companies	Boards; supervisory bodies	Yes
Slovak Republic	**No obligation**			
Slovenia	Gender, Age, Disability, Education, Citizenship	-	-	Indirectly
Spain	Gender, Nationality, Age, Disability	-	-	Yes
Sweden	Gender	"large companies"	Board, CEO and other Executives	Yes
Switzerland	**No obligation**			
United Kingdom	Gender	Firms with more than 250 employees		No

Note: "-"denotes policies are applicable to all companies and positions.

Source: OECD "Diversity at Work" questionnaire.

Data collection is most advanced for monitoring gender imbalances. In Sweden, for example, firms with 10 employees or more are obliged to provide annual reports on pay differences between men and women in similar positions (so-called pay audits). Firms with more than 25 employees have to provide a wage action plan. Similar schemes are in place in Finland and Denmark. In Austria, companies with 150 employers or more also have to provide similar reports, but they are not publically available and need to be kept within the company.

Generally, the availability of employee data on ethnic or migrant background is limited. Only in few countries are employers required to provide data on the nationality of employees. The Netherlands used to monitor ethnic diversity in the workplace under the so-called Wet SAMEN (1998-2003), which required firms with 35 employees or more to provide annual reports on the share of ethnic minorities in the firm (based on country of birth and parental country of birth, excluding Europe), their job levels and diversity policies the firm was implementing.

Overall, the limited evidence renders it difficult to assess whether i) some sectors might be more diverse than others, ii) how women and minorities are faring within companies, iii) whether diversity policies have an impact at the firm level, and iv) whether their effectiveness differs across groups. In addition, results from the HR survey show that only around 50% of firms have assessed the impact of the diversity policies they implemented. Furthermore, among those who had experienced difficulties in implementing diversity policies, 45% stated that measuring their impact was one of the main challenges.

Figure 4.1. Assessment of the impact of diversity measures among firms

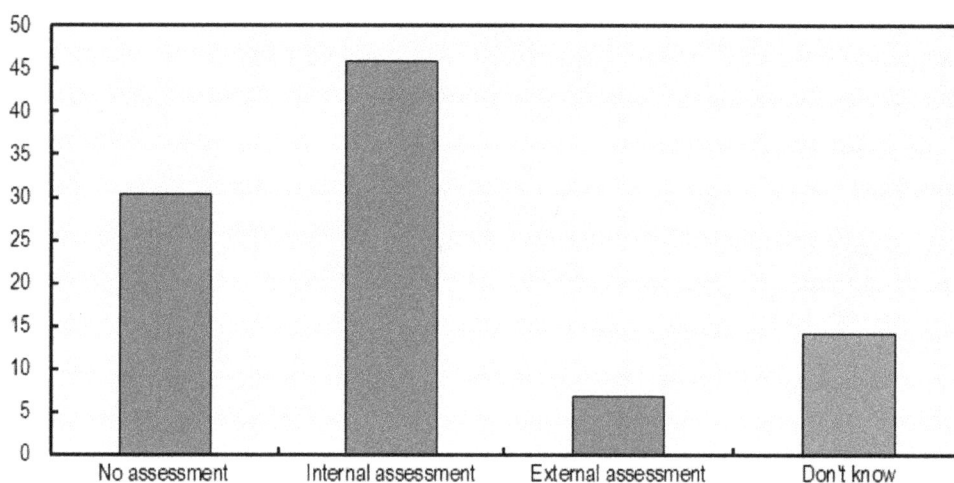

Source: OECD-Dauphine University HR Survey.

In this context, 'knowing what works' and particularly getting a better understanding of how the same policy may affect groups differently, remains a key challenge. At the same time, improving data collection on diversity in the workplace clearly needs to take into consideration concerns around privacy and data protection as well as national legislation around what kind of sensitive data on diversity can be collected. In a context that allows the collection of diversity statistics, this implies that employees cannot be required to provide such data and that privacy is ensured, either through anonymous surveys or – in case data is linked to individual employees – by restricting access to these data only to staff tasked with monitoring.

Finding the balance between firm action and regulatory policy frameworks

Voluntary commitment and active engagement by employers are critical to ensure that diversity policies gain traction, go beyond window dressing and have an actual impact at the firm level. Both in the private and the public sector, employers can take a number of actions that render diversity policies more effective. By their nature, however, such policies rely on the goodwill of companies and therefore can run the risk of not being implemented widely, e.g. when diversity policies are generally not that widespread or well known or when they are seen as controversial. Therefore, it is crucial to determine when legislative frameworks are needed that regulate firm action.

Finding the right balance between voluntary commitments and mandatory policies is a key challenge because it not only requires the 'right mix' of bottom-up and top-down approaches, but also because mandatory policies may have different impacts depending on the type of diversity measure and the group concerned.

For example, quotas for women on boards in Europe were generally found to be effective given the rather strict sanctions that were attached with it, such as having to leave positions vacant. At the same time, the impact of quotas for people with disabilities has been mixed. This is partly due to how they were implemented, e.g. creating additional costs for employers or allowing firms to pay relatively minor fines in case of non-compliance. Thus, the impact of mandatory quotas varies according to groups and strongly depends on how the law is implemented and what sanctions are foreseen.

Furthermore, the impact of diversity policies can also vary across firms. Anonymous application procedures, for example, may be beneficial if there is discrimination in the hiring process. However, in companies that may prefer diverse candidates, anonymous applications can have the opposite result; by redacting candidates' names, age or address, employers are prevented from favouring under-represented applicants when credentials are equal. This shows that implementing such procedures in every employment context is unlikely to have a positive impact, yet it also raises the question of how to determine in which firms such policies would be helpful.

Given that the impact of mandatory policies can differ across groups, firms and types of policies, there cannot be one regulatory policy framework applicable in every context. Therefore, providing general recommendations for when legislative frameworks are needed to regulate firm action is difficult, as such policies are highly context-dependent.

The group-based approach vs. targeting policies

Another issue concerns the design of policies – while evidence points to the importance of closely targeting them to specific barriers faced by women and minorities, there is a limit to how fine-grained these approaches can realistically be.

The group-based approach to diversity and equality, while being the standard approach in OECD countries, may also run the risk of neglecting individuals that happen to fall outside of the groups identified as "diverse". Another issue to consider is that identifying certain groups that are "in need of support" can perpetuate negative stigmas regarding the abilities of women and minorities, which in turn can aggravate their exclusion. For example, research has shown that subsidies which reveal a disability status to potential employers can have a stigmatising effect with regard to their productivity (Deuchert and Kauer, 2017[1]). Similarly, there is a possibility that women in firms with gender quotas are seen as less qualified and only hired because of their gender.

Despite these caveats, targeting diversity policies to group-specific hurdles and needs can still constitute a useful and oftentimes pragmatic policy approach. Considering that a given policy instrument can create different outcomes depending on the group and may even have adverse effects for some, a one-size-fits-all approach may not always work in practice. For example, flexible work arrangements that are only taken up by women because this policy did not include sufficient incentives for male employees may have adverse effects on the long run, e.g. regarding promotions and career advancement.

In addition, while policies would ideally be designed on the granular level, accounting for individual barriers as much as possible, it is clear that targeting is only possible to a certain degree, as such an approach is costly and inefficient. Policies cannot possibly account for all sorts of combinations of disadvantage and may become too narrow to reach a broad audience. Some group-based aggregation, therefore, presents are more efficient and pragmatic approach. Yet striking the right balance can be a challenge; the exact choice of whom to include is debatable and likely depends on the national policy context. Stakeholder engagement is critical to gain a better understanding of the challenges faced by different groups and should therefore systematically include civil society organisations and social partners in the consultation and evaluation process.

Preventing "empty shell" policies

A common criticism is that diversity policies are often adopted as a means for image management and branding, with little regard for their actual impact.[1] The term "empty shell policy" has been coined by Hoque and Noon (2004[2]) to describe the phenomenon that companies have diversity policies on paper, but do not implement them in practice. In an analysis based on the UK Workplace Employee Relations Survey, which is representative by industry and workplaces with 10 or more employees, they observe a gap between espoused, formal written policy and actual practice. Less than half of workplaces with diversity policies in place adopt corresponding supporting practices, e.g. parental leave, nursery, switching from full-time to part-time with regard to women. Moreover, employees often seem to have limited access where such practices do exist and importantly, this access appears to depend on their position in firm hierarchy.

These results are particularly concerning when viewed in light of the finding that the mere existence of diversity structures can induce high-status group members to become less sensitive to unfair treatment. In an experimental study, Kaiser et al. (2013[3]) find that the presence of organisational diversity structures causes high-status group members (White, male employees) to perceive organisations with diversity structures as procedurally fairer environments for underrepresented groups, even when in the experiment it is made clear that underrepresented groups have been unfairly disadvantaged. Managers and high-status employees not only become less sensitive to discrimination of underrepresented groups, but also react more harshly toward underrepresented group members who claim to have been discriminated against. Similar effects are found for judges who are more likely to rule leniently on discrimination cases when companies have diversity policies in place (Edelman et al., 2011[4]). Thus, diversity policies, no matter if mere window-dressing or not, can serve as a legal strategy for firms to shield themselves against claims of discrimination. In addition, assuming a 'good faith' effort also affects women and minorities themselves. In studies with fictional descriptions of firms and law suits, the mere existence of diversity policies in companies decreases women's support for anti-discrimination legislation and their ability to detect sexist behaviour and lead ethnic minorities to assess complaints of discrimination more leniently (Brady et al., 2015[5]; Dover, Major and Kaiser, 2013[6]).

Thus, empty shell policies are not only ineffective in addressing diversity issues, but they may also have a detrimental impact; they can reduce the ability to detect and address persisting issues because the mere existence of diversity policies functions as a reassurance that enough is being done.

While little can be done to change a firm's 'true' motivation, policy design can address a – possibly accidental – implementation of empty shell policies. This includes drawing up comprehensive plans for recruitment, retention and career development with specific, measurable objectives for each step. Such diversity plan are common in the public administrations of many OECD countries (Box 4.1). Monitoring progress over time as well as allocating responsibility for implementation and accountability for outcomes are other critical components to ensure that diversity approaches are more effective (Dobbin and Kalev, 2017[7]).

Evidence on the Dutch Wet SAMEN law has shown that, when employers were required to monitor their workforce and report on measures taken, it was associated with an increase in employment of the target groups (OECD, 2008[8]). This suggests that a mere requirement to report on measures and outcomes can be very effective, as it requires employers to reflect on the issue. Lastly, strengthening internal networks and empowering employees, e.g. through staff networks and mentoring programmes, can support a more bottom-up approach to improve accountability.

Box 4.1. Diversity strategies in the public administration

Public administrations in OECD countries are relatively advanced in establishing comprehensive diversity strategies that comprise the different phases of diversity management (outreach, recruitment procedures, career development). Twelve OECD countries have such government-wide strategic frameworks to foster diversity in the public administration. These strategies are often coordinated by a central HRM body responsible for developing the strategy, monitoring progress, linking diversity issues to strategic workforce planning, and providing guidance and support to public bodies in the implementation process (OECD, 2011[9]). The action plans for such strategies generally:

- establish objectives of what to achieve – generally indicating both broad goals and more specific targets in a comprehensive action plan;
- indicate the target populations, usually including a range of diverse groups;
- outline the tools or means to achieve the targets and realise the vision;
- establish the resources (financial and human) needed to achieve targets;
- and define criteria and processes for the evaluation of policy results.

The implementation of diversity strategies is ensured in different ways. The Spanish government, for instance, has announced special "equality units" tasked with enforcing the diversity strategy in the public administration.

Generally, the enforcement of strategies is based on the principle of "comply or explain". In most countries, publicly accessible reports evaluating the progress on diversity strategies are published. In Austria, ministries have to send a biennial report to the Federal Government indicating if they reached their targets, or else explain why they failed to do so. In Sweden, follow-up on diversity goals is part of senior civil servants' performance review, as well as public agencies' dialogue with the Swedish Agency for Government Employees (SAGE). Other public administrations have elaborate diversity strategies in place, yet without foreseeing concrete enforcement mechanisms.

Promoting diversity policies in SMEs

Diversity policies, and particularly more elaborate diversity strategies, are usually more likely to be implemented by large companies due to larger recruitment needs, bigger HR departments and possibly a stronger interest in branding than it would be the case among small and medium-sized enterprises (SMEs, i.e. companies with under 250 employers). Thus, for SMEs some diversity policies may not be feasible to implement, while for other, less costly approaches, the perception may still be that their implementation is too time-consuming and expensive.

Despite a large selection effect of firms that already have experiences with implementing diversity policies, results from the HR survey indicate that such policies are less common in smaller companies. Around one in three companies with less than 250 employees had implemented diversity policies, compared to around

45% in firms with 250-500 employers and 65% in firms with more than 500 employees. In addition, while around 40% of large companies stated that the topic has gained considerably in importance for them in the past five years, this was only the case among in one in five companies with less than 50 employees.

Despite these obstacles, promoting policies in SMEs is critical; in the OECD, they account for 99% of all firms and around 70% of jobs on average (OECD, 2017[10]). Furthermore, evidence suggests that discrimination tends to be most pronounced in small- and medium-sized companies (SMEs). Possible explanations for this are that these companies face higher stakes when hiring one staff member with an uncertain productivity level, or that SMEs have less experience with diverse workers and are therefore more likely to hold negative stereotypes (Heath, Liebig and Simon, 2013[11]).

While some measures such as outreach campaigns may not be feasible or useful for SMEs, particularly for small and micro enterprises, most diversity policies can in fact be implemented relatively easily as they do not require the introduction of an entirely new policy, but rather an adaptation of existing measures.

For example, recruitment procedures can be adapted relatively cheaply, e.g. by including statements in job descriptions encouraging under-represented groups to apply, not asking candidates for photographs or ensuring more diverse selection committees in interview panels. Furthermore, external partners are critical to support SMEs in implementing diversity policies that require more know-how or larger HR capacity. These can include employers' associations, regional or city-level governments and public employment services as well as NGOs and civil society initiatives, providing, for instance, (online) information and trainings or helping with increasing the talent pool through outreach activities. Such efforts were implemented most strikingly in the Flemish policy of developing so called "Diversity Plans" with SME employers. Support was provided in co-operation with social partners: employer organisations established a "Diversity Service Point" delivering made-to-measure services to support diversity management in SMEs. Trade unions deployed "diversity consultants" who supported staff seeking to establish a diversity policy in their company and who worked closely with SME employers, advising them on how to recruit and make most of diverse workforce. Moreover, SMEs that sought to develop such "Diversity Plans" could request financial support from the Flemish Department of Work and Social Economy (OECD, 2016[12]; van de Voorde and de Bruijn, 2010[13]).

Addressing potential backlash against diversity policies

Addressing pushback against diversity policies and – possibly by extension – negative attitudes towards those targeted by these policies, is a critical step to ensure that diversity can be implemented effectively.

Seeing that in the EU only around one in three would support diversity training, monitoring of recruitment or monitoring of workforce composition in their workforce (Eurobarometer, 2015[14]), both policy makers and employees may have to anticipate adverse reactions when implementing diversity policies. In addition, research suggests that particularly among 'high-status' groups, zero sum beliefs, i.e. the idea that gains of one group necessarily come at the expense of another, are particularly prevalent and can create a sense of losing out or being treated unfairly (Wilkins et al., 2014[15]; Kidder et al., 2004[16]).

Therefore, proactive communication and an adequate framing of diversity is critical to mitigate negative reactions. Framing diversity policies as a means to avoid government sanctions or lawsuits, for example, has shown to lead to more negative reactions than framing diversity policies as part of a management approach that is implemented for business reasons (Kidder et al., 2004[16]). At the firm level, communication around the rationale for diversity policies should therefore emphasise that such policies are not introduced at the expense of other employees and highlight how these are beneficial to the firm overall. Executive leadership is important in this regard, also to highlight the business case. However, a mere top-down approach may also create discontent, particularly when diversity policies are then perceived as a something externally prescribed where staff had little opportunity to provide input. Thus, including staff in the development of such policies, providing opportunities for feedback and listening to concerns may help prevent negative reactions later on.

Proactive communication about the rationale of diversity policies is not only important for firms, but also on a public policy level. Framing diversity policies as one part of social policy, alongside with policies improving access to education, training and jobs, may help to steer a discussion away from 'preferential treatment' and instead move towards a discussion around increasing equality of opportunity for all.

References

Brady, L. et al. (2015), "It's fair for us: Diversity structures cause women to legitimize discrimination", *Journal of Experimental Social Psychology*, Vol. 57, pp. 100-110. [5]

Deuchert, E. and L. Kauer (2017), "Hiring subsidies for people with a disability: Evidence from a small-scale social field experiment", *International Labour Review*, Vol. 156/2, pp. 269-285. [1]

Dobbin, F. and A. Kalev (2017), "Are Diversity Programs Merely Ceremonial? Evidence-Free Institutionalization", in *The Sage Handbook of Organizational Institutionalism*, Sage, London. [7]

Dover, T., B. Major and C. Kaiser (2013), "Diversity initiatives, status, and system-justifying beliefs: When and how diversity efforts de-legitimize discrimination claims", *Group Processes & Intergroup Relations*, Vol. XX/X, pp. 1-9. [6]

Edelman, L. et al. (2011), "When Organizations Rule: Judicial Deference to Institutionalized Employment Structures", *American Journal of Sociology*, Vol. 117/3, pp. 888-954. [4]

Eurobarometer (2015), *Eurobarometer 83.4: Climate Change, Biodiversity, and Discrimination of Minority Groups, May-June 2015*, European Commission. [14]

Heath, Liebig and Simon (2013), *Discrimination against immigrants – measurement, incidence and policy instruments*, OECD Publishing, Paris, https://dx.doi.org/10.1787/migr_outlook-2013-en. [11]

Hoque, K. and M. Noon (2004), "Equal Opportunities Policy and Practice in Britain: Evaluating the "Empty Shell" Hypothesis", *Work, Employment and Society* 3, pp. 481-506. [2]

Kaiser, C. et al. (2013), "Presumed Fair: Ironic Effects of Organizational Diversity Structures", *Journal of Personality and Social Psychology*, Vol. 104/3, pp. 504-519. [3]

Kidder, D. et al. (2004), "Backlash towards diversity initiatives: examining the impact of diversity program justification, personal and group outcomes", *International Journal of Conflict Management*, Vol. 15/1, pp. 77-102. [16]

OECD (2017), *Entrepreneurship at a Glance 2017*, OECD Publishing, Paris, https://dx.doi.org/10.1787/entrepreneur_aag-2017-en. [10]

OECD (2016), *Working Together: Skills and Labour Market Integration of Immigrants and their Children in Sweden*, OECD Publishing, Paris, https://dx.doi.org/10.1787/9789264257382-en. [12]

OECD (2011), *Public Servants as Partners for Growth. Toward a Stronger, Leaner and More Equitable Workforce*, OECD Publishing, https://doi.org/10.1787/9789264166707-en. [9]

OECD (2008), *Jobs for Immigrants (Vol. 2): Labour Market Integration in Belgium, France, the Netherlands and Portugal*, OECD Publishing, Paris, https://dx.doi.org/10.1787/9789264055605-en. [8]

van de Voorde, M. and H. de Bruijn (2010), "Mainstreaming the Flemish Employment Equity and Diversity Policy", in *Equal Opportunities?: The Labour Market Integration of the Children of Immigrants*, OECD Publishing, Paris, https://dx.doi.org/10.1787/9789264086395-10-en. [13]

Wilkins, C. et al. (2014), "You can win but I can't lose: Bias against high-status groups increases their zero-sum beliefs about discrimination", *Journal of Experimental Social Psychology*, Vol. 57, pp. 1-14. [15]

Notes

[1] Similar criticisms have been launched against 'greenwashing' policies that seek to brand a company as environmentally friendly to attract customers, whilst having little or no positive environmental impact.

5 Conclusion

There are several concerns about diversity policies, and indeed ill-designed policies can do more harm than good. A crucial step in addressing public opinion concerns is to clearly communicate that diversity policies do not seek to favour one group over others. To this end, policies must be designed so that they do not primarily benefit those who are already relatively privileged

In many ways, OECD societies and their labour forces have become increasingly diverse over the past decades. How to equip countries to make the most out of this diversity and strengthen equality of opportunity is a key concern for governments, while diversity management is increasingly important for businesses. Ensuring better labour market inclusion of women; immigrants, their descendants and ethnic minorities; LGBT people; older people; and people with disabilities is not only a question of fairness – it is prerequisite for inclusive growth.

In almost one-third of OECD countries, the majority does not believe that their city or local area is a good place to live for ethnic minorities, immigrants or LGBT people in 2018. This share is remarkably stable compared to 2008. While there is cause for cautious optimism with regard to their labour market inclusion (in two out of three OECD countries, employment gaps between men and women and between prime-age and older workers decreased by at least 25% between 2007 and 2017), the pace of this decrease differs markedly across countries. With regard to the gender gap, it has decreased comparatively little in countries with particularly large differences. Furthermore, employment gaps have decreased considerably less for people with disabilities and migrants.

The economic exclusion or inactivity of large population groups evidently comes at a high cost, particularly against the backdrop of demographic ageing and an increasing share of groups that tend to be disadvantaged in the labour market, such as older workers, migrants and ethnic minorities. However, contrary to the often-assumed business case for diversity, the evidence on its impact at the firm level is not that clear-cut. A positive impact is generally found to be higher in knowledge-intensive, high-skilled, and innovation-driven sectors, yet generally, the impact remains small even in these sectors. Likewise, the overall impact of having more foreign-born in the firm or more women on boards on firm performance is small and often insignificant, similarly to the impact of having more diverse teams in the broader workforce.

At the same time, however, research has highlighted the importance of how diversity is dealt with, suggesting that a positive impact of diversity tends to be stronger in firms where diversity is better managed. The idea that diversity needs to be "well-managed" similarly applies at the societal level, where there is some evidence of a negative relationship between higher diversity on the one hand and social cohesion and preferences for redistribution on the other. The observed negative relationship between diversity and social cohesion, however, appears to be largely driven by contextual factors, such as differences in socio-economic status, the level of inequality, lack of social interaction between groups and the role of governance and institutions.

Thus, there is a clear need to strengthen inclusion and better understand under what conditions governments and employers can harness the potential of a diverse workforce more effectively. All 30 OECD countries that participated in the policy questionnaire have some form of diversity policies in place, both for the public and the private sector.

The report has taken a closer look at the effectiveness of six types of diversity policies (non-discrimination legislation, affirmative/positive action, financial incentives, outreach, anonymous applications and diversity training), both because they are widespread and because they are the focus of the existing literature. Overall, however, the evidence base on what works for which groups and why is still limited.

Non-discrimination legislation has been implemented by all OECD countries, often on a wide variety of grounds. While it is difficult to measure its direct effect on improving the labour market inclusion of women and minority groups, there is evidence that legislation can affect attitudes positively by signalling awareness of, and policy attention to, the issue, as well as a general societal shift in norms around equality and equality of opportunity. Furthermore, while the awareness around non-discrimination legislation has increased, in most countries with available data, the majority is not aware of their legal rights in case of discrimination or harassment. Strengthening awareness, along with implementing strong recourse mechanisms for potential victims of discrimination that protect them from retaliation, is therefore critical. However, there is a trade-off to consider here, as non-discrimination legislation can have adverse impacts on protected groups' chances of being hired in the first place, as employers may fear future litigation.

Affirmative action policies (or positive action in the European context) are relatively widespread, either by setting voluntary targets or mandatory quotas. Notably, there has been a proliferation of gender quotas in the European context over the past decade. While such quotas have increased the share of women in executive positions, overall the impact of setting voluntary targets is less clear. They appear to have had a positive impact in the United States, but there is lack of similar evidence for European countries. Furthermore, affirmative action impacts groups differently; evidence from the United States shows that affirmative action in the labour market has benefited white women more strongly than ethnic minorities.

Given that the business case at the firm level is not always clear-cut, financial incentives to hire disadvantaged groups can be a means to strengthen the business case for employers. Evidence suggests that this can be an effective strategy, but only under certain conditions. However, evidence on their impact also shows that getting incentives 'right' is difficult and that such measures must be well-targeted, closely monitored and phased out unless the issues are persistent. Furthermore, public procurement regulations that promote diversity within supplier firms can be an important policy tool to strengthen the business case for diversity and are, in fact, comparatively widespread in OECD countries.

Outreach activities to under-represented groups are another approach that is critical to increase the pool of diverse candidates. Given that groups traditionally disadvantaged in the labour market often lack the necessary professional networks, targeted outreach campaigns should be the first step in a comprehensive diversity strategy. Efforts in this area have notably been made in the public sector.

In addition, there have been a number of pilots assessing the impact of anonymous job applications, redacting, for example, the candidate's name, gender or address. Evidence shows that such anonymous hiring can be an effective tool in some settings, but is impractical for small companies and can be counterproductive in a context where employers actively seek to diversify their workforce.

Lastly, diversity training appears to be the most common diversity practice in the private sector. Yet, for training to be effective it needs to be implemented in a way that avoids backlash – for example, evidence suggests that training should not be framed as a legal obligation imposed on a firm. What is more, positive effects on attitudes dissipate rather quickly. Thus, as a one-time, standalone measure, diversity training is unlikely to have a substantial effect. Instead, it could be seen as a means to get the conversation on existing bias started, but then be combined with other, more structural measures.

Considerable challenges remain in strengthening the impact of diversity policies, both public and private. First of all, data on diversity in the workplace or on the measures taken is limited, which renders policy evaluation difficult and hampers a better understanding of what actually works for which groups and under which circumstances. In addition, finding the right balance between incentivising voluntary commitment by employers and creating policy frameworks that regulate firm action is challenging. This not only requires the 'right mix' of bottom-up and top-down approaches, but also needs to take into account that mandatory policies may have different impacts depending on the type of diversity measure and the group concerned.

Although specific diversity policies are crucial, they often remain stand-alone measures refined to the area of employment or education. Similar to the approach of gender mainstreaming, applying a 'diversity lens' to the preparation and design of policies could therefore ensure that the needs of all groups are addressed in the policy-making process.

Furthermore, there is a risk that diversity policies are adopted as a means for image management and branding, but with little intentions to actually enhance diversity at the workplace. Besides being ineffective, such 'empty shell' policies can actually have a detrimental impact on women and minorities by concealing actual discriminatory practices.

Moreover, implementing comprehensive diversity policies is more common for large companies and the public administration, as they have larger recruitment needs and HR departments. For smaller companies, however, this capacity may not be a given and the (perceived) costs of implementing diversity policies may be too high. Thus, 'getting SMEs on board' is a critical challenge, given that they employ the majority of workers in the OECD.

Lastly, diversity policies are often subject to heated discussion. While there is a large majority of people in the EU agreeing that more should be done to foster diversity at work, only around one in three would be supportive of concrete measures at their own workplace. This indicates that – aside from questions of effectiveness and feasibility – policy makers and employers have to anticipate and manage negative reactions towards diversity policies.

A crucial step in addressing such concerns is to clearly communicate that diversity policies do not seek to favour one group over others. To this end, policies must be designed so that they do not primarily benefit those who are already relatively privileged. Likewise, policy-makers must address the danger that disadvantaged individuals who do not happen to fall into the category of "diverse group" feel left behind. Ultimately, diversity policies can only be one part of a broader package of policies to promote equal opportunities among all members of society.

Annex A. Overview of grounds protected in non-discrimination legislation in OECD countries

Table A A.1. Grounds explicitly protected in non-discrimination legislation

	Gender/Sex	Race	Age	Disability	Sexual Orientation	Religion	Socio-economic status
Australia	▲	▲	▲	▲	▲	▲	
Austria	▲	▲	▲	▲	▲	▲	
Belgium	▲	▲	▲	▲	▲		▲
Canada	▲	▲	▲	▲	▲	▲	
Czech Republic	▲	▲	▲	▲	▲	▲	▲
Denmark	▲	▲	▲	▲	▲	▲	▲
Estonia	▲	▲	▲	▲	▲	▲	▲
Finland	▲	▲	▲	▲	▲	▲	
France	▲	▲	▲	▲	▲	▲	▲
Germany	▲	▲	▲	▲		▲	
Greece	▲	▲	▲	▲	▲		
Hungary	▲	▲	▲	▲	▲	▲	▲
Ireland	▲	▲	▲	▲	▲	▲	
Italy	▲	▲	▲	▲	▲	▲	▲
Japan	▲	▲		▲		▲	▲
Latvia	▲	▲	▲	▲	▲	▲	▲
Lithuania	▲	▲	▲	▲	▲	▲	▲
Luxembourg	▲	▲	▲	▲	▲	▲	
Mexico	▲	▲	▲	▲	▲	▲	▲
Netherlands	▲	▲	▲	▲	▲	▲	
New Zealand	▲	▲	▲	▲	▲	▲	
Poland	▲	▲	▲	▲	▲	▲	
Portugal	▲	▲	▲	▲	▲	▲	▲
Slovak Republic	▲	▲	▲	▲	▲	▲	▲
Slovenia	▲	▲	▲	▲	▲	▲	▲
Sweden	▲	▲	▲	▲	▲	▲	
Switzerland	▲	▲	▲	▲	▲	▲	▲
United Kingdom	▲	▲	▲	▲	▲		
United States	▲	▲	▲	▲	▲		
Total	29	28	26	28	25	24	14

Source: OECD "Diversity at Work" questionnaire.

Annex B. Overview of equality bodies

Table A B.1. Equality bodies that responded to the 2018/19 questionnaire "Diversity at Work", by country

OECD Country	Specialised Equality Body	
Australia	Australian Human Rights Commission	
	Fair Work Ombudsman	
Austria	Federal Equal Treatment Commission	Public administration
	Equal Treatment Commission	Private Sector
Belgium	Institute for the Equality of Women and Men	
	Interfederal Centre for Equal Opportunities (UNIA)	
Canada	Employment and Social Development Canada	
Czech Republic	Public Defender of Rights	
	State Labour Inspection Office of the Czech Republic	
Denmark	Board of Equal Treatment	
Estonia	Gender Equality and Equal Treatment Commissioner	
Finland	Ombudsman for Equality	
	Gender Equality Unit	
Germany	Federal Anti-Discrimination Agency	
Greece	Greek Ombudsman	
Hungary	Equal Treatment Authority	
Ireland	Irish Human Rights and Equality Commission	
Italy	National Equality Councillor	
Japan	Equal Employment Office of the Prefectural Labour Bureau	
Latvia	Ombudsman's Office of the Republic of Latvia	
	State Labour Inspectorate	
Lithuania	Office of the Equal Opportunities Ombudsperson	
Luxembourg	Centre for Equal Treatment	
Mexico	Secretariat of Labor and Social Welfare (PROFEDET)	
Netherlands	Netherlands Institute for Human Rights	
New Zealand	Human Rights Commission	General Human Rights Commission
Poland	Commissioner for Human Rights	
	Government Plenipotentiary for Disabled People	
	Government Plenipotentiary for Equal Treatment	
	National Labor Inspectorate	
Portugal	Commission for Citizenship and Gender Equality	
	Commission for Equality in Labour and Employment	
Slovak Republic	National Centre for Human Rights	
Slovenia	The Advocate of the Principle of Equality	
Spain	Institute for Women	
Sweden	Equality Ombudsman	
Switzerland	Federal Office of Gender Equality	
United Kingdom	Equality and Human Rights Commission	
United States	Equal Employment Opportunity Commission	
	Civil Rights Centre (CRC)	
Total countries: 29	**Total bodies: 40**	

Note: This overview includes all bodies specialised on discrimination issues in the respective country that answered to the recent policy questionnaire administered by the Secretariat.
Source: OECD "Diversity at Work" questionnaire.

Glossary

Disability: A disability reflects any limitation or lack of ability that a person experiences in performing an activity in the manner or within the range considered normal for a person, in other words, a limitation in learning, speaking, walking or some other activity (individual dimension). The definitions and the criteria for determining disability laid down in national legislation and other administrative instances differ widely within OECD member states.

Diversity: Diversity refers to the range of human differences, including but not limited to race, ethnicity, gender, gender identity, sexual orientation, age, social class, religious value systems and national origin.

Ethnic minority: Categories and terminologies vary across countries according to their history, political context and ethnic and racial composition. For example, there are the terms "visible minorities" and Aboriginals in Canada, "ethnic and racial" groups in the United States, "non-Western", "allochtonen" in the Netherlands, "ethnic groups" in the United Kingdom, "people with a migration background" in Germany – the list is extensive and the perspective to adopt any international standard in this matter is probably neither feasible nor appropriate.

Gender: Denotes either of the two sexes (male and female), especially when considered with reference to social and cultural differences rather than biological ones. The term is also used more broadly to denote a range of identities that do not correspond to established ideas of male and female.

Indigenous identity: While no universal definition exists in international law, the term is used to refer to "tribal peoples whose social, cultural and economic conditions distinguish them from other sections of the national community, and whose status is regulated (wholly or partially) by their own customs or traditions or by special laws or regulations" (ILO, 1989).

LGBT: Acronym for lesbian, gay, bisexual and trans people.

Migrant Status: Generally, the status of migrant is defined in different ways in different countries, e.g.: i) someone whose country of birth differs from their country of usual residence; ii) someone whose nationality is not that of their country of usual residence; or iii) someone who has changed his/her country of usual residence for a period of at least a year, so that the country of destination becomes the country of usual residence (United Nations, 1998). For the purposes of this paper, the term migrant status does not make any reference to a person's legal status, but rather refers to the catch-all category of "immigrant" or "foreign born".

Race: In the absence of any internationally agreed definition, race is most often characterised in terms of phenotype and appearance (e.g. skin colours), or with regard to ancestry. Reference to "race" does not entail a belief in the existence of biological races, but is referred to as a "social construct". While some countries have an explicit account of race, in others the terminology avoids the reference to "race", but the content of the category "ethnic origin" is very close to it.

www.ingramcontent.com/pod-product-compliance
Lightning Source LLC
Chambersburg PA
CBHW080339270326
41927CB00014B/3294